CONTENTS

DDOS ATTACK

What it is, and how to stop it

Takehiro Kanegi

Reactive Publishing

PREFACE

In an era where our lives are increasingly intertwined with the digital world, the specter of cyber threats looms large. Among these threats, Distributed Denial of Service (DDoS) attacks hold a particularly insidious place. These attacks, which overwhelm systems with a flood of traffic, can cripple websites, disrupt services, and in some instances, serve as a smokescreen for more nefarious activities. It is within this context that we introduce "DDoS Attack, What It Is and How to Stop One: A Cyber Security Crash Course - Modern Guide." This book is crafted for those who are not newcomers to the realm of cyber security but rather for advanced users who are eager to deepen their understanding of DDoS attacks and fortify their defenses against them.

The purpose of this book goes beyond merely explaining the technical underpinnings of DDoS attacks. Here, we aim to arm our readers with the knowledge and tools necessary to not just comprehend but also effectively counter these digital onslaughts. The text is structured to first lay a comprehensive foundation on what DDoS attacks entail, including their types, methods of deployment, and the psychology driving their perpetrators. From there, we escalate into the more nuanced strategies for mitigation, delving into topics such as real-time monitoring, responsive countermeasures, and the role of artificial intelligence in predicting and preventing attacks.

Our target audience is the seasoned cyber security professional, the network engineer who battles on the front lines of digital defense, and the advanced IT student who yearns to add a critical layer of knowledge to their repertoire. We presuppose a familiarity with basic cyber security concepts, allowing us to delve into more complex and technical discussions without pausing for extensive explanations of fundamental principles.

As you embark on this journey through our guide, we encourage you to approach the material with a critical mind. The landscape of cyber threats is perpetually evolving, as are the technologies and strategies to counter them. This book represents a comprehensive snapshot of the current state of DDoS defense, but it is by no means a static resource. Our discussion is designed to stimulate further exploration, innovation, and dialogue in the field of cyber security.

In this book, chapters are thoughtfully arranged to lead you from the broad strokes into the granular details of DDoS defense mechanisms. Each section builds upon the last, creating a cohesive and comprehensive guide that is not just theoretical but immensely practical. By the end of this text, you will not only understand the "how" of stopping a DDoS attack but also the "why" behind each strategy, equipping you with the knowledge to adapt in the face of new challenges.

"DDoS Attack, What It Is and How to Stop One" is more than a book; it is a clarion call to strengthen our digital defenses against one of the most pressing cyber threats of our time. We invite you to join us in this crucial conversation, to elevate your skills, and to stand as a vanguard in the protection of our digital domain.

CHAPTER 1:
DEFINITION AND
OVERVIEW

The genesis of DDoS attacks lies in the basic principle of overloading a system to the point of inoperation. Imagine a bustling highway; under normal conditions, cars move smoothly, albeit with occasional slowdowns during peak hours. A DDoS attack is akin to suddenly introducing an overwhelming number of vehicles onto this highway, causing gridlock and preventing regular traffic from reaching its destination. In cyber terms, legitimate users are unable to access the information or services they need because the target is too busy handling malicious requests.

DDoS attacks can be broadly categorized into three main types, each with its unique method of flooding targets - volume-based attacks, protocol attacks, and application layer attacks. Volume-based attacks inundate the targeted site with vast amounts of traffic to consume bandwidth. Protocol attacks exploit vulnerabilities in the server's resources, and application layer attacks target web applications with seemingly legitimate requests to overwhelm servers.

Historically, the evolution of DDoS attacks has been closely linked to the expansion of the internet itself. In the early days of the internet, the simplicity and novelty of DDoS attacks made them rare and relatively easy to mitigate. However, as technology advanced, so did the complexity and potency of these attacks. The proliferation of IoT devices, for example, has provided a vast army of potential bots for attackers to exploit due to inadequate security measures.

The ramifications of DDoS attacks are far-reaching, affecting not only the target entity but also the wider ecosystem it operates within. For businesses, a successful DDoS attack can result in significant financial losses, both from the disruption of operations and the cost of mitigating the attack. For governments and critical infrastructure, the stakes are even higher, as such attacks can disrupt essential services and compromise national security.

Understanding the definition and overview of DDoS attacks is crucial for recognizing the severity of these cyber threats and the importance of implementing robust security measures. As we navigate further into the digital age, the role of DDoS attacks in the landscape of cyber warfare is only set to increase, prompting a parallel evolution in defense mechanisms. The following sections will delve deeper into the mechanics of DDoS attacks, their historical context, and the strategies for identification and mitigation, providing a comprehensive guide to combating this pervasive cyber threat.

Explanation of DDOS (Distributed Denial of Service)

Delving into the anatomy of Distributed Denial of Service (DDoS) attacks unveils a complex and methodical approach employed by attackers to incapacitate targeted digital resources. At its foundation, a DDoS attack orchestrates a symphony of compromised systems, known as a botnet, to generate a tsunami of requests aimed at a singular target. The orchestrated assault on the target's infrastructure is meticulously designed to exhaust bandwidth, disrupt services, or degrade the quality of service to the point of inaccessibility for legitimate users.

The construction of a botnet, the primary weapon for a DDoS attack, begins with the infection of multiple systems with malicious software, thereby allowing an attacker to remotely control the compromised devices. These devices can range from personal computers to IoT devices, such as smart refrigerators or CCTV cameras, all co-opted into the botnet without the owners' knowledge. The expansive reach of the internet and the burgeoning IoT landscape have significantly facilitated the proliferation of botnets, making it easier for attackers to amass vast armies of bots.

Once the botnet is established, the attacker can launch a DDoS attack on a target by directing all the bots to send requests to the targeted server or network simultaneously. This sudden surge in requests seeks to overwhelm the target's resources, making it difficult, if not impossible, for the server to respond to legitimate traffic. The sophistication of such attacks lies in their ability to mimic legitimate user behavior, making it challenging for defensive mechanisms to distinguish between benign and malicious requests.

There are several types of DDoS attacks, each exploiting different vectors and methodologies to achieve disruption. For instance, volumetric attacks inundate the target with sheer amounts of traffic, aiming to saturate the bandwidth. Meanwhile, application layer attacks meticulously target specific aspects of a web application or service, requiring fewer resources but demanding more sophistication to carry out effectively. Protocol attacks, on the other hand, exploit weaknesses in the server's infrastructure to consume server resources or disrupt communication between the server and its clients.

The impact of a DDoS attack can be devastating. Beyond the immediate disruption of service and the potential financial repercussions, the longer-term effects can erode trust in a brand or institution, potentially leading to a loss of customers or constituents. Furthermore, DDoS attacks can serve as a smokescreen, diverting attention from more sinister activities such as data breaches or malware installation.

Mitigating the threat of DDoS attacks requires a multifaceted approach. On the technical front, robust defensive measures, including advanced intrusion detection systems, traffic profiling, and web application firewalls, are paramount. Equally important is the cultivation of cybersecurity awareness among stakeholders, ensuring that the basic hygiene of internet-connected devices is maintained to prevent them from becoming part of a botnet.

In the context of the broader cybersecurity landscape, understanding DDoS attacks is not merely about comprehending how they are executed but also recognizing their implications for digital security and governance. As the digital realm continues to expand, the strategies for DDoS mitigation must evolve in tandem, integrating technological advancements and fostering international cooperation to safeguard the integrity of our shared digital infrastructure.

This exploration into the explanation of DDoS attacks underscores the necessity for vigilance and preparedness in the face of evolving cyber threats. As we venture further into this guide, we will dissect the historical context, delve into case studies, and unveil the strategies to identify and combat these insidious attacks, equipping readers with the knowledge to fortify their defenses against the digital onslaught of DDoS attacks.

Differentiating DDOS from DOS (Denial of Service)

In the labyrinth of cybersecurity threats, understanding the nuances between Distributed Denial of Service (DDoS) and Denial of Service (DoS) attacks is crucial for developing effective defense mechanisms. While both strategies aim to disrupt the availability of targeted resources or services, thereby denying legitimate users access, the scale, methodology, and complexity of these attacks differ significantly.

a DoS attack is characterized by its simplicity and direct approach. A single attacker, leveraging one internet connection, attempts to flood a target with excessive requests. This could involve overwhelming a website with traffic or bombarding an email server with messages, thus overloading the server's capacity to process legitimate requests. The simplicity of a DoS attack often means that the tools and techniques required to execute it are less sophisticated, making DoS a common first step for budding cyber miscreants.

In contrast, DDoS attacks represent a more sophisticated evolution of the basic DoS strategy. As the "Distributed" prefix suggests, these attacks harness the power of a botnet—a network of compromised devices, referred to as bots, controlled by the attacker. These devices, which can number in the thousands or even millions, are spread across the globe, making the source of the attack more difficult to identify and mitigate. The distributed nature of a DDoS attack not only amplifies the volume of the assault but also complicates defensive efforts, as the malicious traffic emanates from numerous points across the internet.

One of the critical distinctions between DoS and DDoS attacks lies in their execution. A DoS attack's relatively straightforward nature means it can be launched from a singular location, making it easier for cybersecurity defenses to trace and block the source of the attack. On the other hand, the dispersed structure of a DDoS attack obscures the attack's origin, requiring a more sophisticated and exhaustive defensive approach to distinguish and filter out malicious traffic from legitimate requests.

Furthermore, the barrier to entry for executing DDoS attacks has been lowered by the availability of cheap or even free DDoS-for-hire services and the proliferation of unsecured IoT devices. This accessibility has led to a significant increase in the frequency, complexity, and volume of DDoS attacks in recent years. Attackers can now rent a botnet and launch a substantial DDoS attack without possessing extensive technical knowledge, democratizing the tools of digital disruption to a broader base of individuals with malicious intent.

The motivations behind DoS and DDoS attacks can also vary. DoS attacks are often the work of individual hackers either testing their capabilities or launching targeted attacks against specific entities for personal reasons. DDoS attacks, given their scale, are more frequently associated with organized groups or individuals with significant resources and motivations ranging from financial gain to political statements or even state-sponsored cyber warfare.

The impact of a DDoS attack extends far beyond that of a standard DoS attack due to its ability to disrupt services for extended periods and on a larger scale. The financial and reputational damage inflicted by DDoS attacks can be profound, affecting not only the immediate target but also potentially causing collateral damage to other services and users sharing the impacted infrastructure.

In combating these threats, the differentiation between DoS and DDoS attacks guides the defensive strategies employed. For DoS attacks, traditional firewall and intrusion detection systems may suffice. However, defending against DDoS attacks often requires more complex solutions, including advanced traffic analysis, threat intelligence to anticipate potential sources of attacks, and the deployment of web application firewalls designed to mitigate application layer attacks.

As we delve deeper into the mechanisms and mitigation strategies associated with these attacks, it becomes evident that understanding the distinctions between DoS and DDoS is foundational to fostering robust cybersecurity defenses. The evolution from DoS to DDoS exemplifies the escalating arms race in cyberspace, compelling cybersecurity professionals and organizations to continuously adapt and innovate in the face of these ever-evolving threats.

Historical Context and Evolution of DDoS Attacks

The concept of a Denial of Service (DoS) attack emerged almost as soon as networks did, with the first documented instance occurring in 1974, known as the TCP/IP hijacking. However, the transition from DoS to DDoS, involving the coordinated attack from multiple compromised systems, didn't gain prominence until the late 1990s. The initiation of these distributed attacks marked a significant evolution in the scale and complexity of cyber threats.

One of the landmark events in the history of DDoS attacks occurred in 1996 with the release of the "Trin00" tool, which allowed attackers to exploit multiple systems to launch a unified assault on a single target. This event demonstrated the vulnerability of interconnected systems and the ease with which attackers could amplify their impact by leveraging the distributed nature of the internet.

The late 1990s and early 2000s witnessed several high-profile DDoS attacks that brought the issue to the forefront of cybersecurity discussions. In 2000, major websites including Yahoo!, eBay, and Amazon were brought down by massive DDoS attacks, causing significant financial losses and highlighting the need for robust cybersecurity measures. These early attacks utilized large networks of compromised computers, known as botnets, to flood targets with traffic, a technique that remains a staple in the attacker's arsenal to this day.

As technology advanced, so did the sophistication of DDoS attacks. The mid-2000s saw the emergence of attacks targeting specific vulnerabilities in web applications and infrastructure, such as the exploitation of DNS servers for amplification attacks. These methods allowed attackers to achieve greater disruption with fewer resources, further complicating the challenge for defenders.

The 2010s were marked by an increase in the scale and frequency of DDoS attacks, with incidents regularly making headlines for their impact on government websites, financial institutions, and critical infrastructure. A notable example was the 2016 attack on the DNS provider Dyn, which disrupted access to major internet platforms and services. This attack highlighted the potential for DDoS to not only cause direct damage but also to serve as a distraction for more insidious cyber threats.

Throughout its history, the evolution of DDoS attacks has been characterized by a cat-and-mouse game between attackers seeking to exploit new technologies and defenders striving to secure the ever-expanding digital landscape. The proliferation of Internet of Things (IoT) devices has introduced a vast array of potential bots for DDoS attacks, raising concerns about the future scalability of these threats.

In response to the growing sophistication of DDoS attacks, cybersecurity strategies have also evolved. From the deployment of advanced intrusion detection and prevention systems to the development of decentralized architectures designed to absorb and mitigate attacks, the defense against DDoS requires constant vigilance and innovation.

Reflecting on the historical context of DDoS attacks offers valuable insights into the nature of cyber threats and the necessity for a proactive and collaborative approach to cybersecurity. As we look to the future, understanding the evolution of DDoS attacks empowers us to anticipate and thwart emerging threats, ensuring the resilience and integrity of our digital world.

Mechanisms of a DDOS Attack

At the heart of a DDoS attack lies the principle of inundation. Perpetrators mobilize a multitude of compromised devices, known as a botnet, to generate a flood of traffic directed towards the intended target. These botnets, often comprising thousands of zombified computers or IoT devices, serve as the attack's foot soldiers, executing commands in a synchronized manner to amplify the attack's impact.

The mechanisms of DDoS attacks can be broadly categorized into three types based on the layers of the network they target: volume-based, protocol attacks, and application layer attacks. Each type exploits different aspects of network infrastructure and communication protocols to achieve disruption.

Volume-based Attacks: These are the most straightforward form of DDoS, aiming to consume the bandwidth of the targeted site or service. By generating immense amounts of useless traffic, attackers can saturate the target's connection to the internet, denying access to legitimate users. Techniques such as ICMP floods (ping floods) and UDP floods are common in volume-based attacks, leveraging the simplicity of these protocols to generate high traffic volumes.

Protocol Attacks: This category of DDoS attacks focuses on exploiting weaknesses in the layer 3 and layer 4 protocol stacks to consume server resources or intermediate communication equipment, such as firewalls and load balancers. SYN floods, for instance, exploit the TCP handshake process, creating a backlog of half-open connections that exhaust server resources. Similarly, Ping of Death and Smurf attacks manipulate the protocol's functionality to create disruption.

Application Layer Attacks: The most sophisticated form of DDoS, application layer attacks, target the top layer of the OSI model where web pages are generated on the server and delivered in response to HTTP requests. By mimicking legitimate requests, attackers can exhaust application resources. This category includes HTTP floods and slowloris attacks, designed to slip undetected past security measures, exploiting the specificity of application layer protocols to drain server resources.

The deployment of a DDoS attack follows a multi-stage process, starting with the creation or hijacking of a botnet. Attackers exploit vulnerabilities in devices' software to install malware, bringing the device under their control. With the botnet assembled, the attacker then directs this army of compromised devices to launch coordinated requests towards the target. The cumulative effect of these requests, whether aimed at consuming bandwidth, depleting server resources, or overwhelming application processes, leads to service degradation or complete unavailability.

In addition to direct traffic flooding, attackers often employ techniques to amplify the volume of the attack. DNS amplification, for instance, leverages misconfigured DNS servers to multiply the attacker's request size, increasing the load on the target without a corresponding increase in the attacker's resource expenditure. Similarly, IP spoofing obscures the source of the attack traffic, complicating mitigation efforts and enabling the attacker to bypass some forms of defense.

The mechanisms of DDoS attacks underscore the complexity and adaptability of modern cyber threats. As defenders develop new strategies to mitigate these attacks, attackers evolve their tactics to exploit new vulnerabilities. This ongoing arms race necessitates a comprehensive understanding of DDoS mechanisms, not only for developing effective defense measures but also for anticipating future evolutions of this persistent cyber threat.

The Role of Botnets in Launching Attacks

A botnet is essentially a collection of internet-connected devices that have been compromised by malware, allowing them to be controlled remotely by an attacker or a group of attackers, known commonly as "bot herders." These devices, which can range from personal computers and smartphones to IoT (Internet of Things) devices like smart thermostats or security cameras, are infected and co-opted into the botnet without the knowledge or consent of their owners.

Inception and Growth of Botnets: The formation of a botnet begins with the infection stage, where devices are infected with malicious software through various methods, including phishing emails, malicious advertisements, or exploitation of software vulnerabilities. Once a device is infected, it becomes a "bot," ready to execute the commands of the bot herder. The scalability of botnets is a pivotal aspect of their utility in launching attacks; a botnet can grow to encompass thousands or even millions of bots, creating a formidable force.

Command and Control (C2) Mechanisms: The effectiveness of a botnet in launching coordinated attacks hinges on its command and control architecture. Bot herders communicate with their botnet through C2 servers, issuing commands to launch attacks, spread further infections, or stay dormant to avoid detection. The resilience and redundancy of C2 mechanisms are vital for the longevity of the botnet, with many utilizing peer-to-peer networks or exploiting legitimate services to maintain control over their bots.

Botnets as Tools for DDoS Attacks: When deployed in DDoS attacks, botnets offer attackers the ability to generate overwhelming volumes of traffic from diverse geographic and network origins, complicating mitigation efforts. The distributed nature of botnets means that the attack traffic can appear legitimate, mimicking normal user behavior to evade simple filtering techniques. Furthermore, the sheer scale of botnets allows them to target not just single websites but entire infrastructures, from DNS servers to network bandwidth, with devastating effectiveness.

Amplification and Anonymity: Beyond sheer force, botnets facilitate techniques that amplify the potency of DDoS attacks. For instance, techniques such as DNS amplification exploit the architecture of the internet to multiply the attack traffic, while simultaneously obscuring the origin of the attack, granting attackers a veil of anonymity. By leveraging botnets, attackers can launch potent attacks without a proportional investment in resources, making them a favored tool in the arsenal of cybercriminals.

The Evolving Threat: Botnets are not static threats; they evolve with the cybersecurity landscape. As defenses against DDoS attacks become more sophisticated, so too do the strategies of bot herders. Recent developments have seen botnets exploiting emerging technologies such as AI to identify vulnerabilities more efficiently or automating the spread of malware to expand the botnet more rapidly.

The role of botnets in launching DDoS attacks underscores a critical vulnerability in the fabric of the internet: the security of individual devices. Each device compromised into a botnet represents a failure in cybersecurity practices, whether through unpatched software, weak passwords, or phishing susceptibility. Addressing the threat of botnets, therefore, is not solely a matter of developing more advanced countermeasures against DDoS attacks but also a broader challenge of enhancing the cybersecurity posture of all connected devices.

Types of Attacks: Volume-based, Protocol, and Application Layer Attacks

In the shadowy expanses of cyberspace, Distributed Denial of Service (DDoS) attacks emerge as a prevalent threat, wielding the power to submerge networks under an overwhelming deluge of traffic. DDoS attacks are not monolithic; they manifest in various forms, each designed to exploit different vulnerabilities within a target's digital infrastructure. The primary categories of DDoS attacks - volume-based, protocol, and application layer attacks - reflect the multifaceted nature of this cyber threat, showcasing the ingenuity and malice behind each assault.

Volume-based Attacks: The digital equivalent of blitzkrieg, volume-based attacks, aim to flood the bandwidth of the victim's network with a colossal volume of data. This type of attack is measured in bits per second (bps), signifying the onslaught of traffic that can range from gigabits to terabits, overwhelming network resources and rendering services inaccessible. The ubiquity of such attacks is partially due to their straightforward setup and execution, with attackers often leveraging botnets to amplify the volume of traffic directed at the target. Techniques like UDP flood, where large numbers of User Datagram Protocol (UDP) packets are sent to random ports on a remote host, are common in volume-based attacks, aiming to saturate the bandwidth to a point of total service denial.

Protocol Attacks: Whereas volume-based attacks target the bandwidth, protocol attacks are more insidious, aiming at the server resources and the communication equipment like firewalls and load balancers. These attacks exploit weaknesses in the layer 3 and layer 4 protocol stack to consume disproportionate resources for each request, leading to server or infrastructure failure. A quintessential example is the SYN flood, where a myriad of TCP connection requests overwhelms a server's ability to handle new connections; the attacker sends rapid SYN requests without completing the handshake with ACK responses, exhausting server resources and leading to denial of service. Protocol attacks, measured in packets per second (pps), require a deep understanding of network protocols to execute and mitigate, making them a sophisticated vector of cyber aggression.

Application Layer Attacks: The most cunning among DDoS strategies, application layer attacks, target the layer where web pages are generated on the server and delivered in response to HTTP requests. These attacks are designed to exhaust the resources of the web server itself, often requiring fewer resources to launch but being harder to detect due to their resemblance to legitimate traffic. Tactics such as slowloris, where partial HTTP requests are sent to the server at a slow pace, aim to hold connections open for as long as possible, eventually overloading the server. Application layer attacks, measured in requests per second (RPS), represent a surgical strike against the target, exploiting the nuances of web application behavior to deny service to legitimate users.

Each category of DDoS attack represents a unique challenge for cybersecurity defenses, requiring a nuanced approach to detection and mitigation. Volume-based attacks demand robust bandwidth and filtering mechanisms to absorb and sift through the traffic flood. Protocol attacks necessitate sophisticated rate-limiting and anomaly detection techniques to identify and neutralize abnormal protocol activities. Application layer attacks, with their subtlety and mimicry of legitimate requests, require deep packet inspection and behavioral analysis to discern and defend against. The multiplicity of attack types underscores the necessity for comprehensive cybersecurity strategies that address the full spectrum of potential DDoS vectors.

As the digital landscape continues to evolve, so too do the tactics of those wishing to exploit its vulnerabilities. Understanding the different types of DDoS attacks - volume-based, protocol, and application layer - is fundamental to developing resilient defenses against this ever-present threat. The battle for cybersecurity is waged on many fronts; knowledge of the enemy's arsenal is the first step in fortifying our digital bastions against the relentless tide of DDoS attacks.

How Attackers Exploit Vulnerabilities: Unveiling the Art of Cyber Siege

In the intricate dance of cyber warfare, attackers constantly scout for the Achilles' heel of digital infrastructures, be it in the robust fortifications of enterprise networks or the seemingly inconsequential details of a lone server. Exploiting vulnerabilities, the cornerstone of any successful DDoS attack, involves an acute understanding of the target's weaknesses and the strategic application of pressure where it can cause the most disruption. This exploration delves into the methodologies attackers employ to identify and exploit these vulnerabilities, setting the stage for a catastrophic DDoS onslaught.

Identifying Vulnerabilities: The initial step in the attacker's playbook involves reconnaissance to uncover the chinks in the target's armor. This phase, often executed with meticulous patience, can span from passive activities, such as harvesting publicly available information, to active probing using tools designed to detect open ports, unpatched software, or misconfigured networks. The sophistication of this process can vary, from deploying automated scanning tools that crawl the internet en masse to targeted phishing campaigns aimed at tricking insiders into revealing sensitive information. Through this exhaustive exploration, attackers map out the target's digital landscape, marking points of entry and potential bottlenecks ripe for exploitation.

Exploiting Software Vulnerabilities: With the blueprint of the target's infrastructure in hand, attackers pivot to exploiting known software vulnerabilities. These can range from unpatched operating systems and outdated server software to vulnerable web applications. Tools like SQL injection, cross-site scripting (XSS), and various exploit kits are employed to gain unauthorized access or disrupt services. The attackers' arsenal is constantly updated with the latest exploits, often leveraging zero-day vulnerabilities—flaws unknown to the software vendor or without a patch—for which defense is particularly challenging.

Leveraging Network Infrastructure: Beyond software, the very architecture of the internet and its supporting infrastructure can be turned against its users. Attackers manipulate the way data is routed through the network, using techniques like IP spoofing to masquerade as legitimate traffic, thereby complicating the task of filtering out malicious data packets. Amplification attacks exploit the functionality of open DNS and NTP (Network Time Protocol) servers, turning minor queries into massive responses directed at the unsuspecting target, effectively magnifying the volume of the attack manifold.

Social Engineering: Perhaps the most insidious method of exploiting vulnerabilities lies not in code or hardware but in human psychology. Social engineering attacks, including sophisticated spear-phishing campaigns, prey on the trust and curiosity of individuals to gain access to restricted areas of a network or to deploy malware that facilitates a larger DDoS attack. These techniques underscore the critical importance of cybersecurity awareness and training as part of a comprehensive defense strategy.

Utilizing Botnets: The culmination of exploiting these

vulnerabilities often involves the deployment of botnets, networks of compromised machines harnessed to launch coordinated attacks. By exploiting vulnerabilities across a swathe of devices connected to the internet—ranging from poorly secured IoT devices to unsuspecting users' computers—attackers amass an army capable of launching devastating DDoS attacks. The distributed nature of botnets complicates tracing the attack back to its source, providing attackers with a veil of anonymity.

Understanding how attackers exploit vulnerabilities provides invaluable insights into fortifying cybersecurity defenses. It highlights the necessity of a holistic approach that encompasses not only technological safeguards but also educates and involves every individual within an organization. In the realm of digital security, the maxim "knowledge is power" has never been more apt, as understanding the enemy's tactics equips defenders with the foresight to anticipate and thwart attacks, safeguarding the digital bastions of our interconnected world.

Famous DDOS Attacks and Their Impacts: Chronicles of Digital Havoc

Estonia 2007: The Siege that Shook a Nation: In April 2007, Estonia became the epicenter of a digital assault of unprecedented scale, following a dispute over the relocation of a Soviet-era war memorial. This nation-wide attack crippled government, financial, and media networks, effectively paralyzing the country's digital infrastructure. Beyond the immediate turmoil, the attack marked a seminal moment in cyber warfare, prompting a reevaluation of national security strategies to encompass the digital domain.

Operation Payback 2010: The Swarming of the Digital Hive:

Spearheaded by the hacktivist collective Anonymous, Operation Payback targeted organizations opposing internet piracy, employing DDoS attacks to "punish" companies and legal entities. The assault disrupted the operations of major financial services like Visa, MasterCard, and PayPal, illuminating the power of collective cyber action against institutional entities and setting a precedent for future hacktivist operations.

Dyn 2016: The Day the Internet Stood Still: On October 21, 2016, a massive DDoS attack targeted Dyn, a major DNS service provider, disrupting access to prominent websites including Twitter, Netflix, and The New York Times. Utilizing a botnet comprising millions of IoT devices infected with the Mirai malware, the attackers demonstrated the vulnerabilities inherent in the proliferation of poorly secured internet-connected devices, igniting a global discourse on IoT security.

GitHub 2018: A Record-Breaking Onslaught: In February 2018, GitHub faced a colossal DDoS attack, peaking at 1.35 Terabits per second - the largest such attack recorded at the time. The assault exploited memcached servers to amplify the attack volume, a stark reminder of the evolving sophistication of DDoS methodologies and the need for robust, adaptive defense mechanisms in the face of such threats.

The Impacts: Beyond Digital Disruption: Beyond their immediate operational disruptions, these DDoS attacks underscore broader societal vulnerabilities and the potential for digital sieges to influence geopolitical landscapes, economic stability, and the very essence of how trust is constructed and maintained in digital spaces. The Estonia attack, for instance, catalyzed the establishment of the NATO Cooperative Cyber Defence Centre of Excellence, signifying a shift towards recognizing cyber threats as core national security concerns.

These chronicles of digital havoc serve not merely as cautionary tales but as catalysts for innovation in cybersecurity strategies, resilience planning, and international cooperation. The repercussions of these attacks reverberate beyond their immediate aftermath, challenging us to reimagine our approach to digital defense and to foster a culture of continuous vigilance, preparedness, and adaptability in the face of the ceaseless evolution of cyber threats. Through understanding the impacts of these famous DDoS attacks, we arm ourselves with the knowledge necessary to navigate the turbulent waters of the digital age, ensuring that we can withstand the storms and emerge resilient in their wake.

Analysis of Major DDoS Attacks in History: A Deep Dive into Cyber Siege Tactics

In dissecting the anatomy of pivotal DDoS attacks, we glean invaluable insights into the evolution of cyber siege tactics and the ingenuity of threat actors in exploiting the interconnectedness of the digital realm. This analysis ventures beyond mere chronological recounting, delving into the technical underpinnings, strategic execution, and the multifaceted impacts of these digital onslaughts, offering a granular perspective on their significance in the annals of cyber history.

The Technical Precision of the 2007 Estonia Attack: The Estonia DDoS attacks serve as a masterclass in strategic cyber warfare. Attackers leveraged a constellation of compromised computers to inundate servers with requests, effectively drowning the digital infrastructure of a nation. The technical sophistication lay not just in the scale but in the coordination; the assault was a symphony of malicious traffic directed with precision, exploiting vulnerabilities in network architectures that were ill-prepared for such an orchestrated attack. This incident underscored the necessity for national infrastructures to fortify their cyber defenses and for the development of rapid response mechanisms.

The Mirai Botnet and the Dyn Assault: The 2016 attack on Dyn highlighted a shift in the landscape of DDoS threats—from volume-based to sophistication in execution. The nefarious innovation was the Mirai botnet, an army of enslaved IoT devices. This botnet's ability to direct massive amounts of traffic to Dyn's servers was a wake-up call to the security vulnerabilities inherent in the burgeoning IoT ecosystem. Analysis of the Mirai source code revealed a relatively simple concept executed with devastating effectiveness, leveraging default passwords and widespread device vulnerabilities. The attack catalyzed a reevaluation of IoT security standards and practices, emphasizing the importance of basic security hygiene.

GitHub 2018: Unpacking the Amplification Tactic: The GitHub attack was a stark illustration of amplification techniques in DDoS assaults. Attackers exploited memcached servers— an open-source, high-performance caching system—to amplify their attack bandwidth, achieving unprecedented scale. This technique turned benign servers into unwitting participants in the cyber siege, multiplying the attack volume exponentially. The incident revealed the potential for common networked systems to be turned into force multipliers for DDoS attacks, prompting a reexamination of network configurations and the implementation of safeguards against such misuse.

Evolving Threats and Mitigation Strategies: Across these case studies, a pattern emerges of attackers leveraging the inherent trust and openness of the internet's architecture to mount their offensives. This exploitation of trust underscores the need for a paradigm shift in how digital systems are secured—not just through technological means but through fostering a culture of security awareness and collaboration. The development of DDoS mitigation tools, such as advanced rate-limiting, traffic shaping, and threat intelligence sharing, represents strides toward this goal. Furthermore, the incidents accentuate the importance of collective defense mechanisms and the role of public-private partnerships in enhancing the resilience of the digital ecosystem.

Conclusion: The analysis of these major DDoS attacks underscores the perpetual arms race between cyber defenders and adversaries. Each attack not only tested the mettle of the targeted organizations but also served as a crucible for the cybersecurity community, catalyzing advancements in defensive technologies and strategies. As we reflect on these episodes of digital havoc, the lessons distilled guide us toward a future where preparedness, adaptability, and collaborative defense are the cornerstones of cybersecurity. In dissecting these attacks, we arm ourselves with the knowledge to not only weather future storms but to preempt them, ensuring the integrity of our digital bastions in an ever-evolving cyber landscape.

The Immediate and Long-term Effects on Businesses and Governments: Understanding the Ripple Effects of DDoS Attacks

The aftermath of a Distributed Denial of Service (DDoS) attack unravels in phases, each with its unique spectrum of consequences for businesses and governments. This analysis delves into the immediate and enduring ramifications that these cyber assaults inflict upon their targets, illuminating the diverse ways in which organizations must adapt and fortify themselves against future vulnerabilities.

Immediate Impact on Businesses: The direct fallout from a DDoS attack on businesses is often swift and devastating. Operational disruption tops the list, as services become inaccessible to users, leading to an immediate loss of revenue and erosion of consumer trust. For e-commerce platforms, even a few minutes of downtime can translate into significant financial losses. Additionally, the operational overheads surge as IT teams scramble to mitigate the attack, further straining resources. Beyond the tangible, the reputational damage can be profound and enduring, affecting customer loyalty and brand perception adversely.

Governmental Implications: For government entities, the stakes are uniquely critical. A successful DDoS attack can cripple essential services, from healthcare portals to public safety communication systems, risking lives and public welfare. It can also undermine public confidence in governmental capabilities to safeguard citizens' interests and maintain order. The immediate aftermath often necessitates a rapid response to restore services and a public relations strategy to manage the fallout, demanding considerable resources and attention.

Long-term Business Consequences: Beyond the immediate aftermath, businesses grapple with the long-term implications of a DDoS attack. The erosion of consumer confidence can have lingering effects on market share and growth prospects. The need for increased spending on cybersecurity measures can divert funds from other strategic investments, impacting competitiveness and innovation. Moreover, the potential for increased insurance premiums and the risk of litigation from affected parties can compound financial pressures.

Governmental Long-term Challenges: The challenges for governments extend into the realm of national security and economic stability. Repeated successful attacks can erode a nation's cyber sovereignty, influencing global perceptions of its vulnerability. The economic implications are profound, affecting not just the direct costs of mitigation and recovery but also potentially deterring foreign investment due to perceived cybersecurity risks. Consequently, governments are compelled to enhance their cyber defense mechanisms, often requiring legislative changes, public-private partnerships, and substantial investments in technology and human resources.

Broader Economic and Social Impact: The ripple effects of DDoS attacks on both businesses and governments contribute to a broader economic and social impact. For businesses, the disruption of supply chains and service delivery can have cascading effects on partners, vendors, and consumers, affecting the wider economy. For governments, the impact on critical infrastructure can have significant societal implications, from disrupting education and healthcare to compromising security.

Conclusion: The immediate and long-term effects of DDoS attacks on businesses and governments underscore the multifaceted challenges posed by cyber threats in the digital age. These incidents serve not only as a wake-up call for enhanced cybersecurity measures but also as a reminder of the interconnected nature of modern economies and infrastructures. As organizations navigate the aftermath of these attacks, the lessons learned must inform a proactive approach to cybersecurity, emphasizing resilience, rapid response, and the importance of fostering a culture of security awareness. The path forward involves not just technological solutions but a comprehensive strategy that includes collaboration, legislation, and education to counteract the evolving threat landscape.

Case Studies of How These Attacks Were Executed: Dissecting

the Anatomy of Notorious DDoS Assaults

The digital age, characterized by an ever-expanding online presence, has witnessed a parallel rise in cyber threats, among which DDoS (Distributed Denial of Service) attacks loom large. These cyber assaults, aimed at overwhelming a system's resources to render it unresponsive, have targeted institutions ranging from financial behemoths to governmental agencies. By examining specific case studies, we can glean insights into the execution strategies of these attacks, their objectives, and the lessons learned.

Case Study 1: Operation Ababil - The Assault on U.S. Banks

In 2012, several major U.S. banks, including JPMorgan Chase, Bank of America, and Wells Fargo, faced a series of sophisticated DDoS attacks dubbed "Operation Ababil." These incidents were characterized by their unprecedented scale, employing a network of compromised computers and servers across the globe to flood the banks' websites with traffic. The attackers, a group identifying themselves as the Izz ad-Din al-Qassam Cyber Fighters, purportedly launched these assaults in retaliation for a controversial video that had circulated online.

The banks experienced significant disruptions, with their online services becoming inaccessible to customers for extended periods. The financial sector reeled under the impact, grappling with the dual challenge of restoring services and reassuring jittery customers. The aftermath saw a concerted push towards bolstering cybersecurity defenses, including the establishment of shared threat intelligence networks among banks.

Case Study 2: Dyn DNS Attack - The IoT Botnet Menace

October 2016 witnessed one of the most massive DDoS attacks in history, targeting Dyn, a company that controls much of the internet's domain name system (DNS) infrastructure. This attack utilized a botnet named Mirai, which comprised tens of thousands of compromised Internet of Things (IoT) devices, such as DVRs and surveillance cameras. These devices were infected with malware that allowed attackers to remotely control them, directing an overwhelming volume of traffic towards Dyn's servers.

The impact was widespread, temporarily disabling access to major websites like Twitter, Netflix, and PayPal. The Dyn DNS attack underscored the vulnerabilities inherent in the burgeoning IoT ecosystem and sparked a global discourse on the security of connected devices. It highlighted the necessity for stringent security measures in IoT device manufacturing and the implementation of more robust network infrastructure.

Case Study 3: GitHub Attack - Leveraging Third-Party Services

In 2018, GitHub, the world's leading platform for software development, fell victim to the largest DDoS attack recorded at the time. The assault peaked at an astonishing 1.35 Terabits per second, exploiting memcached servers to amplify the attack's volume. Memcached is a distributed memory caching system, which attackers manipulated by spoofing GitHub's IP address and prompting the servers to flood it with responses.

Remarkably, GitHub's proactive defense mechanisms, including its DDoS mitigation service, managed to thwart the attack within minutes, with minimal disruption to its operations. This incident illuminated the potential for exploiting third-party services in DDoS attacks and the critical importance of real-time, automated defense systems to mitigate such threats effectively.

These case studies of DDoS attacks illustrate not only the diversified tactics employed by cybercriminals but also the evolving landscape of cyber defense. The common thread in each case is the imperative for continuous vigilance, investment in advanced security technologies, and, importantly, collaboration within and across industries to share intelligence and best practices. As the methods of attack grow more sophisticated, so too must the strategies to defend against them. The lessons drawn from analyzing such attacks are invaluable in fortifying our digital defenses and ensuring the resilience of our cyber infrastructure against future assaults.

CHAPTER 2:
IDENTIFYING
DDOS ATTACK

O ne of the harbingers of a DDoS attack is an aberration in network traffic patterns. An unexpected surge in traffic to a particular site or service, especially during off-peak hours, could be the work of an adversary testing the waters before launching a full-scale attack. Monitoring tools can be employed to track these anomalies, setting thresholds that, when exceeded, trigger alerts for further investigation.

As digital storm clouds gather, another telltale sign is an inexplicable degradation in network performance. Users may experience increased latency when accessing websites or services, with pages loading slower than usual or not at all. This deterioration can be the result of a sudden influx of traffic, overwhelming servers and causing delays — a precursor to a more disruptive DDoS attack.

In the lead-up to a DDoS assault, there may be brief, inexplicable outages or disruptions to services. These fleeting disturbances are often a consequence of attackers probing for vulnerabilities, testing their ability to compromise the target's availability.

Such sporadic interruptions should raise red flags and prompt immediate scrutiny of network security protocols.

Scrutinizing server and network logs can reveal unauthorized attempts to access systems or unusual patterns of requests. These logs may contain clues about the origin of the attack, such as a disproportionate number of requests from specific IP addresses or geographic locations. Early identification of these irregularities can be instrumental in thwarting an impending DDoS attack.

Often, the first indicators of network distress come from the users themselves. Complaints about the inability to access services, or reports of unusually slow performance, can be early warnings of a DDoS attack. Establishing a rapid response mechanism for user feedback is essential in identifying and addressing potential threats swiftly.

To effectively counteract the menace of DDoS attacks, organizations must adopt a multifaceted approach. This includes deploying advanced monitoring tools capable of discerning between legitimate traffic spikes and malicious reconnaissance activities. Additionally, implementing a robust incident response plan enables teams to act decisively, minimizing the impact of an attack.

Engaging in regular security audits and fostering a culture of vigilance among staff and users alike can bolster an organization's defenses against these digital tempests. By understanding and recognizing the early signs and symptoms of DDoS attacks, stakeholders can navigate the treacherous waters of cyberspace with greater confidence, ensuring the continuity and reliability of their digital services in the face of adversity.

Unusually Slow Network Performance as a Precursor to DDoS Attacks

Network performance issues can stem from a myriad of benign sources, including routine maintenance, server overloads due to legitimate traffic spikes, or hardware malfunctions. However, when these slowdowns defy logical explanation and persist despite standard troubleshooting efforts, they may signify a deliberate attempt to undermine the network's integrity. DDoS attacks often commence with subtle, low-threshold attacks designed to test the responsiveness and resilience of the target's infrastructure without immediately revealing the attacker's hand.

To comprehend why DDoS attacks specifically result in network slowdowns, one must understand the tactics employed by attackers. By inundating a network with a deluge of superfluous requests across multiple channels, attackers can saturate bandwidth, exhaust server resources, and interfere with legitimate traffic's ability to reach its destination. This orchestrated chaos not only cripples the intended target but can also have a cascading effect on connected services and users, spreading the impact of the attack far beyond its initial scope.

Effective monitoring and diagnostic strategies are paramount in distinguishing between ordinary network performance issues and those indicative of a looming DDoS attack. Employing comprehensive network monitoring tools that analyze traffic patterns in real-time allows for the early detection of anomalies that could precede an attack. These tools can be configured to alert administrators to unusual spikes in traffic or an accumulation of requests from suspicious IP addresses.

In addition to automated monitoring, conducting regular, manual inspections of network performance metrics can uncover subtle irregularities that might otherwise go unnoticed. Techniques such as bandwidth analysis, latency measurement, and packet loss assessment provide a granular view of network health and can unearth the fingerprints of a nascent DDoS campaign.

Recognizing unusually slow network performance as a potential harbinger of a DDoS attack is only the first step. Building a proactive defense necessitates a layered security strategy that includes both technical and procedural elements. Implementing rate limiting, traffic shaping, and IP filtering can mitigate the impact of increased traffic volumes, while a well-orchestrated response plan ensures that teams are prepared to act swiftly and decisively in the face of an attack.

Furthermore, collaboration with Internet Service Providers (ISPs) and cloud-based DDoS mitigation services can extend an organization's defensive perimeter, providing additional layers of protection and resilience. By leveraging the expertise and infrastructure of external partners, organizations can enhance their ability to detect, absorb, and repel DDoS attacks before they reach critical assets.

Unusually slow network performance, often dismissed as a minor annoyance, can be the precursor to a devastating DDoS attack. By recognizing this phenomenon as a potential early warning sign and implementing a robust and proactive cybersecurity posture, organizations can shield themselves from the catastrophic consequences of unchecked DDoS assaults. The battle against DDoS attacks is waged not in the moment of crisis but in the vigilant monitoring and preemptive measures taken to fortify digital defenses against this ever-present threat.

#The Enigma of Site Unavailability: Beyond the Surface of DDoS Attacks

The unavailability of a particular website or the broader inability to access any site can often be traced back to the calculated maneuvers of DDoS attacks. Unlike the blatant onslaught of traffic in more recognized forms of DDoS attacks, some strategies are meticulously designed to fly under the radar, gradually escalating to the point where they render a website inaccessible.

At the heart of these strategies lies the exploitation of vulnerabilities within the network infrastructure, where attackers deploy sophisticated bots to simulate legitimate requests. These bots ingeniously mimic user behavior, making it challenging for traditional security measures to detect and block them without also denying access to genuine users. This subtlety not only maximizes the duration of the attack but also complicates the recovery process.

The implications of a website's unavailability extend far beyond the immediate inconvenience to users. For businesses, it can translate into substantial financial losses, erosion of customer trust, and long-term brand damage. In a realm where milliseconds of downtime can lead to significant competitive disadvantage, the stakes are exceptionally high.

Moreover, the unavailability of critical online platforms, especially those related to financial services, healthcare, and public utilities, can have far-reaching consequences on societal operations and individual well-being. It underscores the broader economic and social vulnerabilities exposed by DDoS attacks, spotlighting the need for a resilient cybersecurity posture.

Addressing the challenge of site unavailability begins with the comprehensive mapping of network architecture to identify potential vulnerabilities that could be exploited by DDoS attacks. This proactive approach, coupled with the deployment of advanced behavioral analysis tools, can significantly enhance the detection of anomalous patterns indicative of a DDoS attack.

Once an attack is detected, immediate mitigation strategies involve the use of web application firewalls (WAFs) and DDoS protection services that can filter out malicious traffic while allowing legitimate users to continue accessing the site. Employing content delivery networks (CDNs) can also distribute the load, reducing the impact on the primary server and ensuring continued availability.

In the quest to safeguard against the unavailability of websites due to DDoS attacks, collaboration emerges as a pivotal strategy. Engaging with peers, cybersecurity experts, and law enforcement can facilitate the sharing of threat intelligence, amplifying collective defense capabilities.

Moreover, establishing partnerships with ISPs and cloud-based DDoS mitigation providers offers an additional buffer, leveraging their expansive infrastructure and specialized expertise to absorb and neutralize threats before they reach the target's network.

The unavailability of a website, whether as an isolated incident or part of a broader pattern of inaccessible sites, serves as a stark reminder of the pervasive risk posed by DDoS attacks in the digital domain. Recognizing this threat and adopting a layered, collaborative approach to cybersecurity can empower organizations to navigate the complexities of DDoS attacks, minimizing their impact and ensuring the continuous availability of critical online services. In the relentless battle against cyber threats, preparedness, resilience, and partnership constitute the triad of a robust defense mechanism.

The Disruption of Connectivity: Dissecting the Role of DDoS in Internet Disconnections

At the core of DDoS-induced internet disconnections is the strategic overload of the target's network bandwidth or resources. By inundating the network with superfluous requests, attackers can exhaust the capacity of the internet connection, rendering it unable to process legitimate traffic. This tactic is not only effective in disrupting the operations of a specific entity but also has the potential to affect the broader network infrastructure, leading to widespread connectivity issues for unrelated third parties.

The methodology behind these attacks varies, with perpetrators often leveraging volumetric attacks to saturate the bandwidth, or more sophisticated layer 7 attacks aimed at depleting server resources with fewer, but more complex requests. Regardless of the approach, the outcome is a pronounced degradation of service or total disconnection for the unsuspecting victims.

The consequences of internet disconnection, particularly when orchestrated through DDoS attacks, extend well beyond the inconvenience of interrupted web browsing or halted online transactions. For businesses, the implications are dire, encompassing operational paralysis, significant financial losses, and a tainted reputation among customers and partners. In today's digital-first world, prolonged internet downtime can be the death knell for online-centric businesses.

On a larger scale, the strategic targeting of critical infrastructure with the intent to disconnect internet services poses a grave threat to public safety, economic stability, and national security. The potential for chaos, should essential services like healthcare, emergency communication, and financial systems be disrupted, highlights the urgent need for robust cybersecurity measures.

Proactive detection and swift response are crucial in mitigating the impact of DDoS-induced internet disconnections. Implementing comprehensive monitoring systems to detect unusual traffic spikes or patterns can serve as an early warning system, enabling preemptive action before connectivity is compromised.

In the event of an attack, having redundancy plans, such as backup internet service providers (ISPs) or failover systems, can ensure continuity of operations. Engaging DDoS mitigation services that can absorb and filter malicious traffic is another critical strategy in safeguarding connectivity.

Beyond technical solutions, fostering a culture of cybersecurity awareness and preparedness across all organizational levels is fundamental. Educating employees about the signs of impending attacks and the importance of security practices can fortify the first line of defense against cyber threats.

The disruption of internet connectivity, whether through wired or wireless connections, serves as a stark illustration of the power and pervasiveness of DDoS attacks in the digital age. Understanding the mechanisms behind these disruptions, their far-reaching consequences, and the strategies for effective mitigation and recovery is essential for any entity navigating the cyber landscape. As the sophistication of cyber threats evolves, so too must our collective resilience and response strategies, underscoring the perpetual arms race that defines cybersecurity.

Unveiling the Arsenal: Advanced Tools for DDoS Detection

DDoS detection tools encompass a broad range of technologies, each tailored to identify the subtle signs of an impending attack. At one end of the spectrum, simple monitoring tools provide basic surveillance over network traffic, flagging abnormal spikes that may indicate a DDoS assault. Though rudimentary, these tools are essential for small-scale operations with limited resources.

Progressing further, we encounter advanced systems imbued with the capability to analyze traffic patterns in real-time. These sophisticated platforms utilize anomaly-based detection methods, leveraging statistical analysis to discern deviations from normal traffic behaviors. By establishing a baseline of regular activity, these tools can detect even the most subtle anomalies indicative of a DDoS attack in its nascent stages.

In addition to anomaly-based detection, signature-based detection plays a pivotal role in identifying DDoS threats. These systems scrutinize traffic for known patterns or 'signatures' associated with DDoS attacks. While highly effective against recognized attack vectors, their dependence on existing knowledge bases renders them less effective against novel or evolving threats.

The advent of machine learning has heralded a new era in DDoS detection capabilities. By harnessing the power of artificial intelligence, detection systems can now learn from past attacks, continuously refining their ability to identify and mitigate threats. These self-learning systems adapt over time, enhancing their proficiency in detecting even the most sophisticated, previously unknown attack patterns.

Given the diverse nature of DDoS attacks, relying on a single detection tool or methodology is insufficient. A multi-layered approach that combines different detection techniques —ranging from basic monitoring to advanced machine learning algorithms—provides a more robust defense. This strategy ensures comprehensive coverage, safeguarding against a wide array of attack vectors and minimizing potential blind spots in defense mechanisms.

Detection is but the first step in a comprehensive DDoS defense strategy. The real-time data and insights garnered from detection tools must be seamlessly integrated with mitigation efforts to effectively neutralize threats. This includes automating responses such as traffic rerouting, rate limiting, or deploying scrubbing centers to cleanse malicious traffic, thereby ensuring minimal disruption to legitimate services.

The arsenal of tools available for DDoS detection is both vast and sophisticated, embodying the frontline defense in the digital battleground against cyber threats. By understanding the functionalities and strategic deployment of these tools, organizations can significantly enhance their resilience against DDoS attacks. As the digital landscape continues to evolve, so too will the tools designed to protect it, promising a future where cybersecurity defenses remain ever vigilant against the tide of cyber aggression.

The Gatekeepers of the Digital Fortress: An Insight into Monitoring Tools and Software

Monitoring software serves a singular, vital purpose: to maintain a constant vigil over network traffic, thereby ensuring the integrity and availability of digital services. These tools are engineered to detect irregularities in data flow, scrutinize packet transmissions, and alert administrators to anomalies that could signify the early stages of a DDoS attack.

The efficacy of monitoring tools hinges on their ability to provide comprehensive visibility into network activities. This includes the tracking of bandwidth usage, analysis of traffic sources, and examination of protocol patterns. By offering a granular view into these elements, monitoring tools empower organizations to swiftly pinpoint and address abnormal behaviors, often before they escalate into full-blown DDoS assaults.

Monitoring solutions can be categorized based on their focus areas and methodologies. Some of the prominent categories include:

- Traffic Analysis Tools: These solutions specialize in scrutinizing the nature and volume of network traffic. Utilizing techniques such as deep packet inspection (DPI), they can differentiate between benign and malicious traffic, providing insights into potential threats.

- Performance Monitors: Focused on the health and efficiency of network systems, these tools track metrics like response times, server load, and uptime. Deviations from baseline performance metrics can indicate disruptions potentially caused by DDoS activities.

- Security Information and Event Management (SIEM) Systems: SIEM systems offer a holistic approach to monitoring. They aggregate and analyze logs from various sources across the network, using correlation algorithms to identify patterns indicative of cyber threats, including DDoS attacks.

The integration of Artificial Intelligence (AI) and automation into monitoring tools marks a significant leap forward in cyber defense capabilities. AI algorithms can process vast datasets, learning from each interaction to better identify the subtle hallmarks of DDoS attempts. This machine learning capability, combined with automation, enables real-time threat detection and response with minimal human intervention. The result is a more dynamic, adaptive approach to DDoS defense, capable of countering the rapid evolution of cyber threats.

Proactive monitoring, the practice of continuous, anticipatory surveillance, offers a strategic advantage in the digital battleground. By employing monitoring tools that not only detect but also predict potential attack vectors, organizations can fortify their defenses well in advance of an actual threat. This anticipatory posture is critical for staying one step ahead of cyber adversaries, ensuring that digital domains remain unbreachable fortresses against DDoS onslaughts.

While monitoring tools and software are formidable in their right, their strength is exponentially amplified when integrated into a broader cybersecurity strategy. This includes the coupling of monitoring insights with robust firewalls, intrusion prevention systems (IPS), and DDoS mitigation services. Such an integrated approach ensures a comprehensive defense mechanism, weaving a tighter security net that leaves little room for cyber threats to penetrate.

Monitoring tools and software are the unsung heroes of the cyber world, tirelessly guarding against the specter of DDoS attacks. Through sophisticated traffic analysis, AI-enhanced detection, and proactive surveillance, these tools play a pivotal role in safeguarding the digital realm. As the complexity of cyber threats continues to evolve, so too must the capabilities of monitoring solutions, ensuring that they remain ever-vigilant sentinels in the ongoing quest for cyber resilience.

Unraveling the Shield: Implementing Anomaly-Based and Signature-Based Detection

Anomaly-based detection stands on the premise of monitoring network activities to establish a benchmark of normal behavior. This approach leverages advanced algorithms and statistical models to continuously analyze network traffic, seeking deviations from established norms. The essence of its functionality lies in its capacity to detect unprecedented or zero-day attacks, making it a vanguard of unknown threat detection.

The implementation of anomaly-based detection involves several key steps:

1. Baseline Establishment: Through the analysis of historical traffic data, a profile of typical network behavior is constructed. This baseline encompasses metrics such as traffic volume, flow patterns, and packet sizes.

2. Real-Time Analysis: The system continuously monitors network traffic, comparing real-time data against the baseline to

identify discrepancies that may indicate malicious activities.

3. Alert Mechanism: Upon detection of an anomaly, the system triggers alerts, providing detailed information about the potential threat. This facilitates swift investigative and remedial actions by cybersecurity personnel.

4. Adaptive Learning: Incorporating machine learning algorithms, anomaly-based systems learn from each detected anomaly, refining the baseline to improve detection accuracy over time.

In contrast to the heuristic approach of anomaly-based detection, signature-based detection operates by identifying known threat patterns or signatures within network traffic. This method is akin to a digital immune system, recognizing the 'signatures' of malware, viruses, and specific attack vectors, including those used in DDoS campaigns.

Key facets of implementing signature-based detection include:

1. Signature Database: The cornerstone of this method is a comprehensive database of known threat signatures, compiled from a plethora of sources, including past attacks, malware samples, and threat intelligence feeds.

2. Continuous Scanning: Network traffic is systematically scanned in real-time, with each packet inspected for matches against the signature database.

3. Immediate Response: Upon detection of a known threat signature, the system can automatically block the offending traffic or isolate the attack, minimizing potential damage.

4. Database Updates: Given the dynamic nature of cyber threats, the signature database requires regular updates to include new threat patterns, ensuring continued efficacy against emerging attacks.

The confluence of anomaly-based and signature-based detection heralds a comprehensive defense strategy. While signature-based detection excels in identifying and neutralizing known threats, anomaly-based detection provides coverage for novel or evolving attacks. Together, they offer a robust shield against a wide spectrum of cyber threats, including the ever-present danger of DDoS attacks.

Implementing a synergistic approach involves:

1. Integrated Systems: Deploying platforms that seamlessly combine both detection methods, offering a unified interface for monitoring and response.

2. Strategic Alert Configuration: Tailoring alert thresholds and responses to balance sensitivity and practicality, minimizing false positives while ensuring real threats are promptly addressed.

3. Continuous Evolution: Leveraging insights from both

detection methods to refine security policies, response strategies, and the overall defensive posture.

4. Cross-Training Teams: Ensuring cybersecurity teams are adept in both detection methodologies, fostering a versatile and dynamic response capability.

In the labyrinthine domain of cybersecurity, where threats morph with alarming rapidity, the dual implementation of anomaly-based and signature-based detection offers a beacon of hope. By judiciously deploying these methodologies in tandem, organizations can significantly enhance their resilience against DDoS attacks and a plethora of other cyber threats, safeguarding the sanctity of their digital assets in this tumultuous era.

Precision in the Shadows: Evaluating the Effectiveness of Intrusion Detection Systems (IDS)

An IDS functions as the digital equivalent of a high-tech surveillance system, meticulously scanning network traffic for signs of unauthorized or suspicious activities. These systems are classified into two primary types: Network-based Intrusion Detection Systems (NIDS) and Host-based Intrusion Detection Systems (HIDS). While NIDS scrutinizes traffic on a network to detect potential threats, HIDS monitors individual devices or hosts within that network. The efficacy of these systems is pivotal in maintaining the integrity and availability of digital resources, rendering their assessment a matter of paramount importance.

The evaluation of an IDS's effectiveness hinges on several key parameters, each contributing to a comprehensive understanding of its capabilities and areas necessitating improvement. This framework encompasses:

1. Detection Accuracy: The ability of an IDS to accurately identify genuine threats while minimizing false positives (erroneous threat alerts) and false negatives (missed threats) is instrumental. High detection accuracy ensures that real threats are promptly addressed without overwhelming security teams with false alarms.

2. Response Time: The velocity at which an IDS can detect and respond to an intrusion attempt directly impacts the containment of potential damage. Rapid response times are critical in mitigating the effects of fast-paced DDoS attacks, where even milliseconds can make a difference.

3. Scalability: As networks expand and evolve, so too must the IDS. Evaluation must consider an IDS's capability to adapt to growing and changing network environments, ensuring continued protection against sophisticated threats.

4. Resource Efficiency: An effective IDS should operate with optimal use of system resources, ensuring that its operation does not unduly burden network or host performance. This balance between vigilance and efficiency is crucial for maintaining normal operations while under the watchful gaze of the IDS.

5. Integration Capacity: The ability of an IDS to integrate seamlessly with other security tools and systems enhances its effectiveness. This includes compatibility with firewalls, antivirus software, and security information and event management (SIEM) systems, creating a cohesive and fortified defense structure.

6. User Interface and Management: The utility of an IDS is

also measured by the intuitiveness of its interface and the ease with which it can be managed and configured. A user-friendly interface coupled with comprehensive management tools empowers security professionals to tailor the system to meet specific security needs.

Evaluating the effectiveness of an IDS entails a multifaceted approach, incorporating both quantitative and qualitative analyses:

- Simulated Attack Scenarios: Conducting controlled attacks, including DDoS simulations, to test the IDS's detection and response capabilities under various conditions.

- Benchmarks and Standards: Utilizing established benchmarks and industry standards to measure performance and compliance with best practices.

- Peer Reviews and Case Studies: Analyzing feedback from peer reviews and case studies to gain insights into the IDS's performance in real-world scenarios.

- Continuous Monitoring and Auditing: Implementing ongoing monitoring and auditing processes to assess the IDS's effectiveness over time, adapting to new threats and technologies.

The thorough evaluation of Intrusion Detection Systems is a cornerstone of cybersecurity strategy. By rigorously assessing detection accuracy, response time, scalability, resource efficiency, integration capacity, and user interface management, organizations can ensure that their IDS not only meets current security requirements but is also poised to evolve with the dynamic landscape of cyber threats. In doing so, they fortify their defenses against the relentless onslaught of attacks, including the pervasive threat of DDoS attacks, safeguarding the digital realm with unwavering vigilance and precision.

The Art of Cyber Resilience: Responding to an Attack

The first moments following the detection of a cyber attack are critical. They set the tone for either a successful mitigation or a catastrophic breach. For DDoS attacks, where the attacker floods the network with traffic to disrupt service, the response time can significantly influence the attack's impact.

1. Traffic Analysis and Identification: The initial step involves analyzing the incoming traffic to differentiate between legitimate user requests and malicious DDoS packets. Advanced filtering mechanisms and rate limiting can be employed to stem the tide of fake requests.

2. Activation of a Response Plan: Having a predefined DDoS incident response plan allows for a swift and organized reaction. This plan outlines the roles and responsibilities of the response team, communication protocols, and step-by-step mitigation strategies.

3. Engagement of Mitigation Services: Many organizations enlist the aid of DDoS mitigation services that specialize in absorbing and dispersing malicious traffic. The immediate engagement of these services can be crucial in defending the network's integrity.

4. Communication: Clear and timely communication with stakeholders, including employees, customers, and partners, is essential. This transparency helps manage expectations and reduces the potential for panic and misinformation.

As the attack unfolds, the focus shifts to sustaining operations and minimizing damage. This involves a series of tactical maneuvers aimed at outmaneuvering the attackers.

1. Application of Rate Limiting: Implementing rate limiting on critical resources helps ensure that services remain available to legitimate users, even under attack.

2. Traffic Re-routing: Utilizing content delivery networks (CDNs) and redundant network paths can help dissipate the attack's force, rerouting malicious traffic away from critical assets.

3. Update and Adjustment of Filters: As the attack progresses, attackers may alter their strategies. Continuously updating filtering criteria to block new attack vectors is vital for maintaining defensive postures.

The aftermath of a cyber attack offers invaluable lessons and insights into strengthening future defenses.

1. Comprehensive Attack Analysis: Conducting a detailed review of the attack, including the methods used, the response's effectiveness, and any system vulnerabilities exploited, is crucial for learning from the incident.

2. Revision of Response Plans: Based on the attack analysis, revising and updating the incident response plan to address any weaknesses or oversights ensures better preparedness for future incidents.

3. Strengthening System Defenses: Implementing stronger security measures, such as enhanced encryption, more robust

authentication processes, and advanced anomaly detection systems, can fortify defenses against subsequent attacks.

4. Engagement in Cybersecurity Community: Sharing insights and learnings from the attack with the broader cybersecurity community can help others prepare and defend against similar threats, fostering a collective resilience.

Responding to a cyber attack, particularly a DDoS assault, demands a blend of immediate action, strategic maneuvering, and post-event reflection. By adopting a comprehensive response strategy that encompasses immediate mitigation efforts, tactical defenses during the attack, and thorough analysis and reinforcement afterward, organizations can navigate the complexities of cyber warfare. This approach not only minimizes the damage inflicted by an attack but also enhances the organization's overall cybersecurity posture, turning challenges into opportunities for growth and fortification.

The First Line of Defense: Initial Steps When Under Attack

The genesis of an effective defense against a DDoS attack lies in the rapid identification and assessment of the assault. Recognizing an attack in its infancy involves monitoring for sudden spikes in traffic, unusual patterns of requests, and the performance degradation of services. Tools that offer real-time analytics and alert systems are indispensable allies in this endeavor.

1. Activation of Incident Response Team: The moment an attack is identified, the incident response team must be mobilized. This team, a group of individuals with specialized roles and responsibilities, serves as the command and control center to

orchestrate the defense efforts.

2. Initial Damage Assessment: An early assessment helps to gauge the attack's scale, targeted services, and potential impact. This information is crucial for prioritizing response efforts and resources.

In the shadow of a cyber onslaught, clear, concise, and continuous communication emerges as a cornerstone of effective crisis management.

1. Internal Coordination: Immediate communication within the organization ensures that all departments and individuals are aware of the situation, understand their roles, and are prepared to act in concert with the response plan.

2. External Notification: Promptly informing external stakeholders, including customers, suppliers, and partners, about the attack and its potential effects on services helps manage expectations and maintains trust. Transparency is key, albeit with a caution not to disclose details that could further compromise security.

With the gears of the response plan grinding into motion, deploying technical countermeasures to blunt the force of the attack is imperative.

1. Traffic Filtering and Rate Limiting: Employing traffic filtering to block malicious data packets and rate limiting to control incoming requests can significantly reduce the attack's effectiveness, allowing legitimate traffic to continue.

2. Utilization of Redundant Networks and Services: Leveraging

redundant network paths and cloud-based services can help dissipate the attack's impact, ensuring some level of service continuity.

3. Engagement with Intrusion Detection Systems: Intrusion detection systems (IDS) can analyze traffic patterns in real-time, helping to identify and isolate malicious packets, further mitigating the attack's impact.

The initial phase of responding to a DDoS attack concludes with a reassessment of the situation. This involves a review of the effectiveness of the deployed countermeasures and an evaluation of the ongoing risk. Based on this reassessment, adjustments to the response strategy may be necessary to bolster defenses and mitigate the attack more effectively.

1. Feedback Loop: Establishing a feedback loop within the incident response team ensures that insights gained from the initial response can be quickly integrated into ongoing defense strategies.

2. Preparation for Escalation: In the event that the attack escalates, being prepared to implement more drastic measures, such as completely isolating affected systems or seeking external assistance from cybersecurity firms, is vital.

The initial response to a DDoS attack is a crucible in which the metal of an organization's cybersecurity posture is tested and tempered. By swiftly identifying the attack, effectively communicating within and outside the organization, deploying immediate technical countermeasures, and continuously reassessing the situation, an organization can establish a formidable first line of defense. This not only mitigates the immediate threat but also sets the stage for a resilient and robust long-term defense strategy, turning adversity into an opportunity to strengthen cyber resilience.

Navigating the Storm: Communication Protocols with Your ISP

Before the tempest of a DDoS attack breaks upon digital shores, the groundwork for effective communication must be laid. Establishing a dedicated line of communication with your ISP is not merely a preparatory measure but a strategic investment in resilience.

1. Designated Contacts: Identifying and establishing contact with designated representatives within your ISP ensures that in times of crisis, communication is streamlined, direct, and devoid of unnecessary bureaucratic delays.

2. Understanding ISP Protocols: Familiarizing yourself with the ISP's protocols for handling DDoS attacks lays the foundation for a coordinated response effort. This includes understanding the types of mitigation services offered, response times, and escalation procedures.

As the digital squall of a DDoS attack intensifies, the symbiotic relationship between an organization and its ISP transitions from preparatory to active defense. This phase is characterized by shared intelligence, coordinated strategies, and mutual support.

1. Real-Time Information Sharing: Providing your ISP with real-time analytics and data concerning the attack facilitates a more nuanced and effective mitigation response. This data exchange should focus on the nature of the traffic, identified patterns, and the attack's vector.

2. Joint Mitigation Efforts: ISPs possess a broader perspective and access to more extensive resources for DDoS mitigation. Collaborating on a mitigation strategy can leverage these resources, including rerouting traffic, employing scrubbing centers, and applying advanced filtering solutions.

3. Adjustment and Adaptation: The dynamic nature of DDoS attacks necessitates a flexible response strategy. Continuous communication between an organization and its ISP enables both parties to adapt their defense mechanisms in real-time, countering the evolving threat landscape.

The aftermath of a DDoS attack offers a unique temporal space for reflection, analysis, and fortification against future assaults. In this phase, communication shifts towards a post-mortem analysis and strengthening of preventive measures.

1. Post-Attack Review: Conducting a joint review of the attack with your ISP can uncover valuable insights into the attack's dynamics, effectiveness of the response, and areas for improvement. This collaborative review fosters a deeper understanding and prepares both parties for future adversities.

2. Upgrading Defense Strategies: Based on the insights gained, organizations can work with their ISPs to implement advanced defense strategies, refine existing protocols, and explore new technologies or services designed to bolster resilience against subsequent attacks.

3. Regular Communication and Updates: Maintaining an ongoing dialogue with your ISP ensures that your defensive

posture evolves in tandem with the changing cyber threat landscape. Regular updates, shared best practices, and continued education on emerging threats solidify the partnership and defense readiness.

In the shadow of the burgeoning threat posed by DDoS attacks, the partnership between an organization and its ISP transcends a mere vendor-client relationship, morphing into a dynamic alliance against a common adversary. Through proactive establishment of communication channels, collaborative defense efforts, and a commitment to post-crisis fortification, this alliance becomes a cornerstone of digital resilience. The narrative of combating DDoS attacks is thus not solely about technological prowess but equally about the strategic symphony orchestrated between an organization and its ISP, a partnership that turns the tide in the ceaseless battle for cybersecurity.

Legal and Ethical Considerations in the Face of DDoS Attacks

The battle against DDoS attacks is not waged in a lawless void. Various international and national laws provide a legal scaffold for both preemptive action against and reaction to DDoS attacks. Understanding these laws is paramount for ensuring that defensive measures do not inadvertently cross legal boundaries.

1. Cybercrime Legislation: Many countries have specific legislation that criminalizes the execution of DDoS attacks, such as the Computer Fraud and Abuse Act (CFAA) in the United States. Entities must familiarize themselves with such laws to understand the legal context of DDoS mitigation.

2. Data Protection Regulations: Efforts to mitigate DDoS attacks often involve the processing of vast amounts of data, some of which may be personal. Regulations like the GDPR in the

European Union impose strict guidelines on data handling, emphasizing the need for compliance in DDoS defense strategies.

3. Cooperation with Law Enforcement: In the aftermath of a DDoS attack, navigating the requirements and procedures for cooperating with law enforcement is vital. Legal statutes often outline specific obligations for reporting and assisting in the investigation of cybercrimes.

Beyond the letter of the law, ethical considerations play a crucial role in shaping the response to DDoS attacks. The decentralized and often international nature of these assaults raises questions about the ethical use of countermeasures, the responsibility towards unaffected third parties, and the ethics of retribution.

1. Proportionality of Response: The principle of proportionality must guide the deployment of defensive technologies. Measures that might cause collateral damage to innocent third parties, such as overly aggressive IP blocking or counter-attacks, demand careful ethical consideration.

2. Privacy Concerns: The ethical obligation to protect user privacy intersects with DDoS mitigation efforts. Even in the pursuit of security, the principles of necessity and minimal data exposure must remain paramount.

3. Transparency and Accountability: Ethical practice demands transparency about security incidents and accountability for the measures taken in response. This includes clear communication with users about potential data risks and the steps taken to mitigate those risks.

Establishing a proactive ethical framework is essential for

navigating the legal and moral complexities of DDoS defense. This involves creating clear policies, engaging in stakeholder dialogue, and ensuring continuous ethical training for cybersecurity teams.

1. Ethical Guidelines: Developing comprehensive ethical guidelines for DDoS response strategies helps in maintaining a moral compass and provides a reference point for decision-making during crises.

2. Stakeholder Engagement: Dialogue with stakeholders, including customers, employees, and peers, fosters a broader understanding of the ethical implications of DDoS defense measures and promotes a culture of ethical awareness.

3. Ongoing Training: Regular training sessions on the legal and ethical aspects of cybersecurity enable teams to stay informed about the evolving landscape and ensure that their actions align with both legal mandates and ethical norms.

The path to defending against DDoS attacks is fraught with legal hurdles and ethical quandaries. By grounding their strategies in a thorough understanding of the relevant legal frameworks and adhering to a strong ethical code, organizations can navigate these challenges with integrity. In doing so, they not only protect their digital assets but also contribute to the fostering of a secure, resilient, and ethically sound cyberspace. This commitment to legal compliance and ethical conduct forms the bedrock upon which effective and responsible DDoS mitigation strategies are built.

CHAPTER 3: THE TECHNICAL SIDE OF DDOS ATTACKS

I n a digital age where connectivity and online presence form the backbone of our societal structure, the integrity and authenticity of our communications have become paramount. IP spoofing, a technique shrouded in the darker veils of cyber manipulation, stands as a testament to the complexities and vulnerabilities inherent within our networked world.

IP spoofing is the creation of Internet Protocol (IP) packets with a forged source IP address. This practice is employed with the intent to conceal the identity of the sender or to impersonate another computing system. This deception forms the crux of numerous cyberattacks, including some of the most sophisticated Distributed Denial of Service (DDoS) onslaughts witnessed by the cyber realm.

The process of IP spoofing involves the deliberate manipulation of packet headers. An attacker modifies the source address in the packet header to make it appear as though the packet is coming from a trusted, legitimate source. This is akin to sending a letter with a falsified return address. The primary objective is to deceive the receiver about the origin of the message, thereby bypassing IP address-based security measures.

Consider a scenario where an attacker aims to breach a networked system that employs IP whitelisting—a method where only certain predefined IP addresses are allowed access. By spoofing the IP address of a whitelisted entity, the attacker can gain unauthorized entry into the system, potentially unleashing a plethora of malicious endeavors.

DDoS attacks, characterized by their aim to overwhelm a target with a flood of internet traffic, often employ IP spoofing as a tactical maneuver. Here, the attacker directs a multitude of compromised systems to send traffic to a single target. By spoofing the IP addresses of these systems, the true source of the attack is concealed, complicating the defense process and making it challenging to block the incoming traffic without also blocking legitimate users.

An illustrative example of this can be seen in the attack on Dyn, a major DNS provider, in 2016. The assault led to widespread internet disruption, affecting services like Twitter, Netflix, and PayPal. The attackers used a botnet composed of a multitude of IoT devices, with spoofed IP addresses masking the botnet's involvement and making mitigation efforts arduous.

While IP spoofing presents a formidable challenge, several strategies can fortify defenses against it:

1. Packet Filtering: Implementing stringent packet filtering rules can help identify and block packets with suspicious, mismatched, or anomalous header information.

2. Ingress and Egress Filtering: This involves monitoring and

controlling the flow of traffic entering and exiting a network. By ensuring that outgoing packets have a source IP address within the valid range for the network, and that incoming packets are from expected, legitimate sources, networks can reduce the risk of spoofed packets.

3. Authentication: Employing authentication mechanisms can ensure that the sender of a message is who they claim to be, offering a robust defense against spoofing attempts.

In the context of Vancouver, a city reputed for its tech-savvy populace and innovative tech scene, local anecdotes suggest that small and medium-sized enterprises (SMEs) have been particularly vigilant in implementing such defenses. By fostering a culture of cybersecurity awareness and adopting proactive security measures, these businesses have been able to mitigate the risks posed by IP spoofing.

IP spoofing remains a significant threat in the landscape of cybersecurity, underpinning many of the sophisticated attacks that target the very fabric of our digital infrastructure. However, by understanding its mechanics, implications, and by implementing robust defenses, we can shield our networks from the perils it poses. Through education, vigilance, and technological innovation, we can turn the tide against those who seek to exploit the vulnerabilities within our systems, ensuring a safer and more secure digital future.

What is IP Spoofing and How It Facilitates DDoS Attacks

IP spoofing, in essence, involves masquerading one's IP address to impersonate another, forging the digital identity of devices across the network. By manipulating the IP header of packets sent across the network, attackers create a facade, using it to mask their true location and intentions. This subterfuge is not merely about anonymity; it's a tool wielded to breach trust, to deceive and manipulate systems into believing in a false origin of traffic.

The deceptive simplicity of IP spoofing belies its potential for havoc, particularly in the orchestration of DDoS attacks. Here, the attacker leverages a network of compromised devices, known as a botnet, to flood a target with traffic, aiming to overload and incapacitate it. IP spoofing adds a layer of complexity to this attack vector, making it arduous for the targeted entities to discern and filter out malicious traffic from legitimate requests.

For instance, consider a DDoS attack targeting an online retailer. The attacker employs a botnet, directing a deluge of requests at the retailer's server. By spoofing the IP addresses of these requests, the attack's origin becomes obfuscated, rendering traditional IP-based blocking techniques ineffective. The retailer's servers, unable to cope with the onslaught, become overwhelmed, leading to service disruptions and potentially significant financial and reputational damage.

A nefarious use of IP spoofing within DDoS attacks is in the amplification of the attack volume. Attackers target vulnerable servers, such as those running the Domain Name System (DNS) service, sending requests with spoofed return addresses. These servers, deceived by the spoofed addresses, send responses to the unsuspecting targets. The voluminous, unsolicited responses amplify the traffic flood, exacerbating the attack's impact. This technique not only leverages the bandwidth of the compromised servers but also magnifies the attack's force, all while masking the true perpetrators.

In a landmark event, GitHub found itself at the receiving end of a massive DDoS attack, notable not just for its scale but for the sophistication of its execution. The attackers harnessed a botnet to send spoofed queries to third-party servers, which then unwittingly bombarded GitHub with data. This exploit of the Memcached system turned ordinary servers into unwitting participants in a colossal attack, demonstrating the potent combination of IP spoofing and DDoS tactics.

Combating IP spoofing and its role in facilitating DDoS attacks demands a multifaceted approach. Beyond the deployment of ingress and egress filtering, there is a pressing need for the adoption of more advanced techniques such as anomaly detection systems that can discern patterns indicative of spoofed traffic. Moreover, collaboration among ISPs to implement anti-spoofing protocols and share intelligence on emerging threats can significantly hinder attackers' ability to leverage IP spoofing in DDoS attacks.

IP spoofing, with its ability to obfuscate and deceive, plays a pivotal role in the orchestration of DDoS attacks. It challenges the foundational trust on which the internet operates, turning the network's openness against itself. As we venture further into the digital age, understanding and countering this tactic is paramount in the ongoing battle to secure cyberspace. Through technological innovation and collaborative efforts, we can erect barriers against this shadowy threat, safeguarding our digital frontiers from the chaos sown by IP spoofing and DDoS attacks.

Methods Used to Prevent IP Spoofing

Ingress filtering stands as a primary bulwark against IP spoofing. Implemented at the network's edge, this technique scrutinizes incoming packets, comparing their source addresses with a database of legitimate IP addresses within the network's purview. Packets bearing source addresses that fall outside of acceptable parameters are promptly discarded. This method, though straightforward, effectively curtails the influx of spoofed packets, thereby blunting the edge of potential DDoS assaults.

Complementing ingress filtering, egress filtering exercises vigilance over outbound traffic. By ensuring that all outgoing packets bear source IP addresses valid within the network's domain, egress filtering prevents the network from being co-opted as a pawn in an attacker's scheme. This dual approach of ingress and egress filtering forms a foundational defense, safeguarding the integrity of both internal and external network traffic.

The adoption of Best Current Practice 38 (BCP 38) offers a comprehensive framework for IP spoofing mitigation. BCP 38, also known as Network Ingress Filtering, provides guidelines for ISPs to implement robust filtering policies. By rigorously applying these practices, ISPs can significantly diminish the efficacy of IP spoofing tactics, thereby contributing to the broader effort to stem the tide of DDoS attacks.

The implementation of encrypted authentication mechanisms, such as TLS (Transport Layer Security) and SSL (Secure Sockets Layer), further reinforces defenses against IP spoofing. By establishing a secure and authenticated channel of communication, these protocols ensure that entities on either end of a connection are genuinely who they purport to be. This authentication process, predicated on cryptographic principles, offers a robust countermeasure against the masquerade of IP spoofing.

Advancements in anomaly detection systems herald a new era in the fight against IP spoofing. Leveraging machine learning algorithms, these systems scrutinize network traffic patterns, identifying deviations indicative of spoofing activities. Once flagged, these anomalies can be isolated and analyzed, enabling timely intervention before a potential DDoS attack can gain momentum.

In the realm of cybersecurity, unity breeds strength. Collaborative efforts among organizations and ISPs to share intelligence about emerging threats and vulnerabilities play a critical role in pre-empting IP spoofing attempts. Platforms such as the Information Sharing and Analysis Centers (ISACs) facilitate this exchange, bolstering collective defenses across the digital landscape.

Consider the scenario within the financial sector, where transactions necessitate the highest levels of security. Encrypted authentication protocols such as SSL ensure the legitimacy of both parties in a transaction, mitigating the risk of IP spoofing. This security measure is instrumental in safeguarding sensitive financial data and maintaining the integrity of online transactions.

The battle against IP spoofing is waged on multiple fronts, encompassing a spectrum of strategies from basic filtering techniques to advanced cryptographic measures. As cyber adversaries evolve, so too must our defenses. The meticulous implementation of these methods, coupled with a commitment to collaboration and innovation, paves the way towards a future where the threat of IP spoofing, and by extension DDoS attacks, is significantly diminished. Through diligence and adaptability, we fortify our digital bastions, ensuring the continued security and resilience of our cyber domains.

Impact of IP Spoofing on the Effectiveness of DDOS Attacks

IP spoofing serves as a catalyst in the amplification of DDoS attack volume. Attackers exploit vulnerabilities in large networks, directing traffic to a target under the guise of legitimate IP addresses. This not only multiplies the attack's force but also obscures the assailant's identity, complicating efforts to trace and neutralize the threat. For example, in reflection attacks, attackers send requests to third-party servers with spoofed IP addresses, causing the servers to flood the unsuspecting victim with overwhelming responses.

The deceptive nature of IP spoofing complicates the task of distinguishing legitimate traffic from malicious payloads. Traditional security mechanisms often rely on IP address reputation systems to filter out potential threats. However, by masquerading as a trusted IP, attackers bypass these defenses, rendering them ineffectual. This evasion tactic prolongs the duration of the DDoS attack, increasing its potential to inflict damage.

IP spoofing enables attackers to rope unsuspecting third-party servers into their DDoS campaigns. By spoofing the IP address of the target, attackers direct traffic from these servers to the victim, exploiting them as unwilling accomplices. This not only magnifies the attack but also implicates these third-party servers in the assault, further muddying the waters of attribution.

To counteract the enhanced threat posed by IP spoofing in DDoS attacks, a multi-faceted approach to cybersecurity is imperative. The deployment of advanced intrusion detection systems capable of identifying anomalous traffic patterns is crucial. Furthermore, the implementation of stringent network access controls, such as source IP verification, can significantly reduce the efficacy of IP spoofing tactics. Additionally, ongoing collaboration between ISPs to share threat intelligence and refine IP filtering techniques stands as a bulwark against these sophisticated attacks.

The Mirai botnet attack of 2016, one of the most potent DDoS attacks in history, leveraged IP spoofing to harness a vast army of IoT devices. These devices bombarded DNS provider Dyn with traffic, leading to significant disruptions across major websites. The incident underscores the imperative for robust security protocols capable of thwarting IP spoofing techniques, highlighting the need for continuous innovation in cybersecurity defenses.

The symbiotic relationship between IP spoofing and DDoS attacks creates formidable challenges for cybersecurity practitioners. The ability of IP spoofing to magnify the scope, scale, and elusiveness of DDoS attacks necessitates a vigilant and adaptive security posture. Through the diligent application of advanced detection methodologies, rigorous network hygiene, and collaborative threat intelligence sharing, the cybersecurity community can mitigate the impact of these threats. As we navigate the ever-evolving landscape of cyber warfare, the resilience of our networks against IP spoofing and DDoS attacks will be paramount in safeguarding the integrity of our digital world.

The Role of Botnets in DDoS Attacks

A botnet, essentially a network of compromised computers, is remotely controlled by an attacker, known as the botmaster. These infected machines, often referred to as zombies, form a digital army that can be mobilized to execute coordinated attacks across the internet. The process of creating a botnet begins with the dissemination of malicious software, typically through phishing emails, malicious websites, or exploiting vulnerabilities in unsecured devices. Once a device is compromised and brought under the control of the botmaster, it can be used not only to perpetrate attacks but also to spread the malware further, thereby expanding the botnet.

The power of a botnet in the context of DDoS attacks lies in its ability to generate massive volumes of traffic from multiple sources. When directed towards a single target, this deluge of requests can overwhelm servers, leading to service disruptions or complete shutdowns. Botnets allow for the execution of various types of DDoS attacks, including but not limited to TCP/UDP flood attacks, HTTP flood attacks, and amplification attacks. Each of these utilizes the botnet's extensive reach to inundate the target with more traffic than it can handle, exploiting different aspects of the network's communication protocol to maximize disruption.

The Mirai botnet provides a stark illustration of the destructive potential of botnets harnessed for DDoS attacks. Comprised of millions of IoT devices such as digital cameras and DVR players, Mirai was used to execute some of the largest and most disruptive DDoS attacks ever observed. One of its notable victims was the service provider Dyn, which experienced widespread service disruption across its managed DNS infrastructure, impacting major internet platforms and services. Mirai's effectiveness was largely due to its exploitation of default usernames and passwords on IoT devices, highlighting the importance of basic security practices in preventing botnet recruitment.

The fight against botnets requires a multi-pronged approach, involving the coordination of individuals, organizations, and governments. Key strategies include securing devices through regular software updates, changing default credentials, and employing firewalls and antivirus tools. At the network level, anomaly detection systems can identify and mitigate unusual traffic patterns indicative of a DDoS attack. Furthermore, legislation and law enforcement play critical roles in disrupting botnet operations, through the takedown of command and control servers and the prosecution of botmasters.

As technology evolves, so too do the strategies employed by cybercriminals. The emergence of 5G networks and the ever-expanding universe of IoT devices offer new opportunities for botnet expansion, underscoring the need for ongoing vigilance and innovation in cybersecurity measures. By understanding the mechanisms underlying botnet-facilitated DDoS attacks, the cybersecurity community can develop more effective defenses against these insidious threats, safeguarding the digital landscape for all users.

botnets represent a significant threat in the realm of cybersecurity, particularly in their capacity to execute devastating DDoS attacks. Through a combination of technological safeguards, legislative action, and public awareness, it is possible to stem the tide of botnet proliferation and protect against the damage they can inflict. The battle against botnets and DDoS attacks is ongoing, requiring the concerted effort of the global cybersecurity community to ensure the safety and reliability of our digital infrastructure.

How Botnets Are Formed and Controlled

The inception of a botnet begins with the recruitment of bots, a task accomplished by exploiting a variety of vulnerabilities found in devices connected to the internet. Cybercriminals deploy malware through a plethora of vectors, including phishing campaigns, malicious software downloads, and exploiting vulnerabilities in IoT devices or outdated systems. Once a device is infected, it becomes a bot, surreptitiously awaiting commands from its new overlord, the botmaster.

A vivid example of this recruitment process can be seen in the Conficker worm. Utilizing a vulnerability in the Windows operating system, Conficker infiltrated millions of computers worldwide, creating a massive botnet. Its proliferation was so rampant that it prompted the formation of a global coalition aimed at halting its spread.

After recruitment, the next phase involves the botmaster taking control of the bots. This is achieved through command and control (C&C) channels, which can be centralized, decentralized, or based on a peer-to-peer structure, depending on the botnet's architecture. Centralized models rely on direct communication between the botmaster and bots via specific servers, while decentralized and peer-to-peer models afford more anonymity and resilience against takedown efforts.

For instance, the Zeus botnet, known for its role in stealing banking information, utilized a centralized C&C mechanism. Law enforcement agencies' eventual takedown of Zeus' C&C servers underscores the vulnerability of centralized botnets to disruption.

The dark web plays a significant role in the formation and control of botnets, serving as a marketplace for selling botnet kits and hiring botnet services. These markets allow even those with minimal technical know-how to commandeer their own botnet, lowering the entry threshold for engaging in cybercriminal activities. The commodification of botnet resources on the dark web illustrates the evolving landscape of cybercrime, where tools and services are traded openly among criminals.

Cybercriminals employ various strategies to fortify their botnets against dismantling efforts. Techniques such as fast-flux DNS and domain generation algorithms (DGAs) are used to rapidly change the IP addresses and domain names associated with C&C servers, complicating efforts to track and neutralize the botnet. Additionally, some botnets are designed to automatically update their malware code to evade detection by antivirus software, further ensuring their longevity.

Combating the formation and control of botnets necessitates a multifaceted approach. Enhancing device security through regular updates, employing robust antivirus solutions, and educating users on the risks of phishing are foundational steps. On a broader scale, international cooperation among law enforcement, cybersecurity firms, and ISPs is essential for identifying and dismantling C&C infrastructure.

the formation and control of botnets underscore the persistent threat posed by cybercriminals in the digital age. By dissecting these processes, cybersecurity professionals can better anticipate the evolving tactics of attackers and fortify defenses accordingly. The battle against botnets is dynamic, requiring constant vigilance, adaptation, and collaboration across the cybersecurity ecosystem to mitigate their impact.

The Scale of Botnets and Their Capabilities in DDOS Attacks

Botnets operate by co-opting a multitude of infected devices, known as bots, to perform coordinated actions at the behest of an attacker. The scale of these networks can range from a few thousand to several million compromised devices. The Mirai botnet, for instance, demonstrated the potential for immense scale by exploiting insecure Internet of Things (IoT) devices. At its peak, Mirai controlled over 600,000 bots, launching devastating DDoS attacks that disrupted major internet platforms and services across the United States and Europe.

The principal strength of botnets in DDoS attacks lies in their ability to aggregate the bandwidth and processing power of countless bots, directing this collective force against targeted servers or networks. Such attacks can inundate the victim with overwhelming volumes of traffic, exceeding their capacity to respond or function. A poignant example of this capability was witnessed in the attack against Dyn, a company that controls much of the internet's domain name system (DNS) infrastructure. This assault not only crippled Dyn but also impacted access to major websites like Twitter, Netflix, and PayPal, showcasing the cascading effects of botnet-powered DDoS attacks on connected ecosystems.

Botnets are not monolithic in their approach to DDoS attacks; rather, they employ a spectrum of strategies to exploit different vulnerabilities. Volume-based attacks, such as UDP floods, aim to saturate the bandwidth of the target, while protocol attacks, like SYN floods, exhaust server resources by initiating incomplete connection requests. Additionally, application-layer attacks target specific aspects of a website or application, aiming to crash the service with seemingly legitimate requests. The versatility and adaptability of botnets in executing these varied attack types make them particularly perilous adversaries.

One of the most sophisticated uses of botnets in DDoS attacks involves amplification techniques, where attackers exploit the normal functionality of protocols to magnify the volume of traffic directed at the target. The 2016 attack on the website of journalist Brian Krebs serves as a hallmark example, where attackers used a botnet to amplify traffic by a factor of 50-70 times, resulting in an attack strength of 620 Gbps. This method demonstrated not only the raw power of botnets but also the cunning ingenuity in exploiting network protocols for malicious purposes.

Addressing the scale and capabilities of botnets in DDoS attacks requires a concerted effort from individuals, organizations, and governments. Strategies include securing IoT devices, implementing advanced threat detection systems, and fostering international cooperation to disrupt botnet C&C infrastructure. Moreover, leveraging cloud-based DDoS mitigation services can offer scalability and flexibility in defending against attacks of significant magnitude.

In essence, the battle against botnets and their capabilities in DDoS attacks is a continuous struggle in the cybersecurity domain. As botnets evolve, so too must the tactics and technologies employed to neutralize them. Understanding the scale and modus operandi of these digital leviathans is the first step in fortifying defenses and ensuring the resilience of critical infrastructure in the face of burgeoning cyber threats.

Strategies for Dismantling or Mitigating Botnets

The proliferation of insecure IoT devices has significantly facilitated the expansion of botnets. A fundamental strategy for combating this trend is the rigorous application of security practices in the design and manufacture of IoT devices. This includes the implementation of strong default passwords, regular firmware updates, and the capability for users to easily modify security settings. For instance, after the Mirai botnet's devastating impact, manufacturers began to prioritize security features, leading to the development of IoT devices less susceptible to hijacking.

Advancements in machine learning algorithms have opened new avenues for detecting and neutralizing botnets before they can launch large-scale attacks. By analyzing network traffic patterns and identifying anomalies, these systems can flag potential botnet activity. Google's use of machine learning to detect botnet activity across its platforms demonstrates the potential of AI-driven approaches to pre-emptively disrupt botnets' communication and coordination capabilities.

Sinkholing refers to the redirection of traffic from infected devices (bots) to a controlled server (sinkhole) that prevents the bots from reaching their intended malicious targets. This not only disrupts the botnet's operations but also allows for the identification of affected devices. For example, the global effort to combat the Conficker worm involved the use of sinkholes to significantly reduce the worm's spread and impact.

Law enforcement agencies and cybersecurity firms often collaborate in concerted efforts to dismantle botnets. These operations typically involve taking control of the botnet's command and control (C&C) servers and subsequently shutting them down. A notable case was the takedown of the Avalanche network, which served as a platform for numerous malware campaigns. The operation involved international cooperation and led to the arrest of key figures behind the network, showcasing the effectiveness of legal and technical collaboration in combating botnets.

Botnets do not respect national boundaries, making international cooperation crucial for effective mitigation.

Strengthening legal frameworks to facilitate the sharing of information and collaborative takedowns is essential. The Budapest Convention on Cybercrime serves as a prime example of an international treaty aimed at combatting cybercrime, including botnet-related offenses, through harmonized legal measures and enhanced cooperation among signatory states.

Cloud-based DDoS mitigation services offer scalable solutions to protect against botnet-driven attacks. By diffusing traffic across a global network of servers, these services can absorb and mitigate the impact of volumetric attacks. Companies like Cloudflare and Akamai have successfully mitigated massive DDoS attacks, illustrating the cloud's role as a bulwark against botnet aggression.

Dismantling or mitigating botnets demands a cohesive strategy that integrates technological advances, operational tactics, legal measures, and international collaboration. While the threat posed by botnets is formidable, the ongoing evolution of cybersecurity practices provides a beacon of hope. As the global community continues to refine and implement these strategies, the resilience of our digital infrastructures against the scourge of botnets will only strengthen, safeguarding the integrity of our interconnected world.

Application Layer Attacks: Unveiling the Stealthy Threat

Unlike the broad, brute-force approach characteristic of traditional network layer attacks, application layer attacks are insidious, focusing on specific applications. The HTTP/HTTPS layers that facilitate web traffic become the battlegrounds. These attacks are not merely disruptive; they aim to manipulate the application's functionality, often leaving the underlying network infrastructure untouched and unsuspecting of the chaos unfolding at the surface.

Consider the case of an SQL Injection, a prevalent form of application layer attack. By inserting malicious SQL queries into an input field, an attacker can manipulate a website's database, leading to unauthorized access to sensitive data. The infamous 2019 attack on a major financial institution, leading to the exposure of personal information of millions of customers, underscores the devastating potential of such vulnerabilities when exploited.

What sets application layer attacks apart is their ability to mimic legitimate traffic, making detection particularly challenging. They exploit specific vulnerabilities in applications, such as inadequate input validation, to execute arbitrary commands or access unauthorized data. This stealthy approach allows them to fly under the radar of traditional security measures focused on volumetric threats.

The sophisticated nature of application layer attacks necessitates advanced detection techniques. Traditional security mechanisms, geared towards identifying sudden surges in traffic indicative of DDoS attacks, often fail to flag these subtle intrusions. The need for deep packet inspection and anomaly detection algorithms becomes evident, highlighting the shift towards more intelligent and adaptive security solutions.

Mitigating application layer attacks requires a multifaceted approach, emphasizing both prevention and real-time response mechanisms.

The foundation of a robust defense strategy lies in secure coding practices. Developers must be vigilant, adhering to coding standards that prioritize security, such as input validation, to minimize vulnerabilities that can be exploited.

Web Application Firewalls (WAFs) play a pivotal role in shielding applications from attacks. By analyzing HTTP/HTTPS traffic, WAFs can detect and block malicious requests before they reach the application. The dynamic nature of application layer attacks, however, necessitates that WAFs are continually updated to recognize the latest threats.

Emerging technologies in behavioral analysis and machine learning offer promising avenues for enhancing detection capabilities. By learning the normal behavior of applications, these systems can identify deviations indicative of an attack, enabling timely interventions. The successful mitigation of a sophisticated application layer attack targeting a renowned e-commerce platform, without disrupting genuine user transactions, illustrates the efficacy of leveraging machine learning in cyber defense.

Application layer attacks pose a formidable threat to the sanctity of web applications, exploiting the very functionalities designed to facilitate user interaction. Their stealth and specificity demand a defense strategy that is both comprehensive and adaptive, integrating secure coding practices, advanced detection technologies, and the vigilant deployment of WAFs. As cyber threats continue to evolve, so too must our defenses, ensuring the integrity and availability of the digital services that have become integral to our daily lives.

Detailed Examination of Attacks on the Application Layer: Unraveling the Complex Web

Application layer attacks, by their very design, target the services that are closest to the end-user. This includes web pages, APIs, and protocols such as HTTP, HTTPS, FTP, and DNS among others. The attackers' modus operandi involves exploiting flaws in the application's logic, authentication mechanisms, and data handling processes to achieve their malicious objectives.

Take, for instance, Cross-Site Scripting (XSS), where attackers inject malicious scripts into content viewed by other users. An example that stands out is the breach of a popular social media platform, where attackers exploited an XSS vulnerability to hijack users' sessions, compromising personal information.

Another perilous vector is Cross-Site Request Forgery (CSRF), which tricks the victim's browser into executing unauthorized actions on a website where they are currently authenticated. A notorious case involved a banking application where attackers induced multiple transactions without the users' consent or knowledge.

The subterfuge integral to application layer attacks involves a detailed reconnaissance phase where attackers meticulously identify potential vulnerabilities, such as weak spots in input validation or outdated application components. Following this, the actual exploitation takes place, which could range from data theft and session hijacking to complete system compromise.

A recurring theme in many application layer attacks is the exploitation of inadequate input validation mechanisms. Attackers craft input data that the application is not programmed to anticipate or handle gracefully, leading to undesirable outcomes such as SQL injections or buffer overflows. A striking example includes a major data breach resulting from an injection flaw in a commercial website's search functionality, leading to the leak of millions of customer records.

In the perpetual arms race that is cybersecurity, evolving threats necessitate dynamic and resilient defensive strategies. Protecting the application layer demands a holistic approach, marrying both preventative measures and real-time detection capabilities.

A proactive stance involves adopting secure coding practices from the ground up. Application developers must be attuned to security considerations, incorporating input validation, parameterized queries, and encoded output to thwart potential attack vectors.

The deployment of application-level intrusion detection systems (IDS) marks a critical line of defense. These systems scrutinize every aspect of incoming and outgoing application traffic, employing heuristic and signature-based detection methods to identify anomalous patterns indicative of an attack.

An illustrative case study involves a high-profile e-commerce platform that faced a sophisticated application layer attack aiming to disrupt its payment gateway. By leveraging an IDS combined with a machine learning algorithm, the platform was able to detect unusual transaction patterns and isolate malicious requests, effectively mitigating the attack with minimal disruption to genuine users.

As the digital landscape continues to evolve, so too does the sophistication of threats aimed at the application layer. These attacks present a clear and present danger to the integrity, confidentiality, and availability of online services. Through a detailed examination of these threats, their mechanisms, and the vulnerabilities they exploit, organizations can arm themselves with the knowledge and tools necessary to fortify their defenses. In this ongoing battle, vigilance, education, and innovation stand as our best allies in safeguarding the digital frontiers.

How These Attacks Differ from Network Service Attacks: Dissecting the Layers

At the heart of network service attacks lies the objective to compromise the availability, integrity, and confidentiality of network resources. Unlike their application-layer counterparts, these attacks primarily target the infrastructure and protocols that facilitate network communication.

A quintessential example of network service attacks, DoS and DDoS aim to overwhelm a network's bandwidth or resources, rendering services inaccessible to legitimate users. These attacks exploit vulnerabilities in network protocols or flood the network with excessive requests. A landmark case was the attack on a major DNS provider, which disrupted internet access across the United States by leveraging a massive network of compromised IoT devices.

MitM attacks intercept and manipulate communications between two parties without their knowledge. This could involve eavesdropping on sensitive information or injecting malicious data into the communication stream. An illustrative instance occurred when attackers compromised a public Wi-Fi network, intercepting financial transactions of users connected to the network.

Application layer attacks, in contrast, exploit vulnerabilities within the software applications themselves. These attacks are more subtle and sophisticated, aiming to manipulate application logic, steal data, or compromise user sessions directly.

While network service attacks often rely on brute force to disrupt services, application layer attacks are characterized by their stealth and precision. For example, SQL Injection exploits poorly designed web application databases by injecting malicious SQL queries. This method was used in a renowned attack to siphon millions of records from a prominent retail chain's database.

The defense strategies for these categories of attacks must be as distinct as their methodologies.

Protecting against network service attacks involves securing the infrastructure through measures such as robust firewalls, anti-DDoS solutions, and secure network protocols. Regularly updating and patching network equipment also play a critical role in thwarting these attacks.

Mitigating application layer attacks demands a focus on secure coding practices, regular application security assessments, and the deployment of web application firewalls (WAFs). Educating developers about secure coding techniques and common vulnerabilities is also crucial.

Consider the case of a multinational corporation that faced both a DDoS attack on its network infrastructure and a subsequent application layer attack targeting its customer database. The DDoS attack was mitigated by rerouting traffic through a cloud-based DDoS protection service, effectively absorbing the malicious traffic. In contrast, the application layer attack required an extensive audit of the application's codebase, the implementation of input validation and parameterized queries, and the deployment of a WAF to prevent future incidents.

The battle against cyber threats requires a deep understanding of the enemy's tactics. By dissecting the fundamental differences between application layer attacks and network service attacks, organizations can tailor their defense strategies to encompass the full spectrum of potential vulnerabilities. This comprehensive approach is not only about deploying the right tools but also cultivating a culture of security awareness and resilience that adapts to the ever-evolving landscape of cyber warfare. Through detailed examination and strategic preparedness, the digital domain remains a fortress amidst the ceaseless waves of cyber assaults.

Defense Mechanisms Against Application Layer Attacks: Fortifying the Final Frontier

Before diving into the defense mechanisms, it's imperative to understand the nature of the beast. Application layer attacks exploit specific vulnerabilities in applications to either steal data, disrupt service, or execute unauthorized actions. Common examples include Cross-Site Scripting (XSS), SQL Injection, and Cross-Site Request Forgery (CSRF).

The first line of defense against application layer attacks begins at the development phase. Implementing secure coding practices can effectively nullify many of the vulnerabilities that attackers exploit. Regular code audits and adherence to secure coding standards (such as OWASP's Top Ten) are crucial. For instance, input validation can prevent SQL Injection attacks by ensuring that only sanctioned input is processed by the application.

A Web Application Firewall (WAF) operates as a gatekeeper

between internet traffic and the web application, analyzing HTTP requests for malicious content. By deploying WAFs, organizations can filter out nefarious data packets before they reach the application. Customizable rulesets enable the blocking of known attack vectors and can be tailored to the specific security needs of the application.

Ongoing security assessments, including penetration testing and vulnerability scanning, are vital in identifying potential weaknesses within an application's framework. A real-world example of this proactive approach was seen when a major financial institution engaged ethical hackers to test their systems, uncovering a critical vulnerability that, if exploited, could have exposed sensitive customer data.

Robust authentication and authorization mechanisms ensure that only legitimate users can access an application and perform actions within their permission levels. Implementing multi-factor authentication (MFA), role-based access control (RBAC), and session management can significantly reduce the risk of unauthorized access.

Encrypting sensitive data, both in transit using protocols like TLS and at rest, shields it from prying eyes, even if other security measures are bypassed. An illustrative case is a healthcare provider that encrypted patient records, ensuring confidentiality even in the event of a data breach.

A well-defined Application Security Incident Response Plan (ASIRP) equips organizations to rapidly respond and mitigate damages in the wake of an attack. This plan entails clear protocols for incident identification, containment, eradication, and post-incident analysis.

The defense against application layer attacks demands a comprehensive and proactive security strategy. By integrating secure coding practices, deploying advanced security tools like WAFs, and continuously evaluating the application's security posture, organizations can build a resilient defense against these sophisticated threats. Moreover, fostering a culture of security awareness and preparedness among developers and IT staff further strengthens the organization's cybersecurity framework. As attackers evolve, so too must our defenses, adapting to counter new threats with innovation, diligence, and a commitment to safeguarding our digital frontiers.

CHAPTER 4:
PLANNING AND
PREVENTION

R isk assessment, the bedrock upon which cybersecurity defenses are built, begins with identifying the assets most valuable to an organization. These treasures range from tangible assets like servers and network infrastructure to intangible assets such as customer data and intellectual property. Each asset, akin to a unique piece of a puzzle, requires specific protection measures to guard against the multifaceted threats it faces.

The next phase involves threat modeling, a process reminiscent of a grandmaster envisaging moves on a chessboard. Here, the potential adversaries are profiled, from script kiddies wielding automated tools to state-sponsored hackers with arsenals capable of orchestrating sophisticated DDoS attacks. Understanding the adversary's capabilities, motivations, and potential attack vectors is paramount in anticipating and preparing for impending assaults.

Vulnerability analysis sheds light on the chinks in the armor —flaws in software, misconfigurations in network devices, and lapses in security protocols that could be exploited by attackers. Tools and techniques, ranging from automated scanners to meticulous manual testing, play a pivotal role in uncovering these weaknesses.

The culmination of this process is the risk matrix—a tableau that prioritizes risks based on their likelihood and potential impact. This prioritization is crucial, for it guides the allocation of resources, ensuring that the most critical vulnerabilities are fortified first.

With the chessboard set, strategic planning commences, a meticulous process that involves drafting a comprehensive defense strategy against DDoS attacks. This strategy is a tapestry woven with multiple threads—technical defenses, procedural policies, and response protocols, each vital to the integrity of the cybersecurity framework.

Technical defenses are the bulwarks and battlements that shield against the onslaught of DDoS attacks. These include network architecture designed for resilience, with redundancy and failovers that ensure continuity of service amid an attack. Advanced DDoS mitigation tools and services, such as cloud-based protection platforms, offer a dynamic shield, adapting to the ever-changing tactics of adversaries.

Procedural policies, the codex of the realm, dictate the actions and responsibilities of the guardians of the digital fortress. These policies encompass regular security audits, ensuring that defenses are not just static edifices but are continually fortified and evolved. Employee training programs are the crucible where the sentinels are forged, imbuing them with the knowledge to recognize and repel threats.

Response protocols are the battle plans, laid out in advance, detailing the course of action in the event of a DDoS attack. These protocols include communication strategies, both internal and with external entities such as ISPs and cybersecurity firms, ensuring a coordinated and swift response to mitigate the impact of the attack.

Risk assessment and planning are the shield and the sword in the battle against DDoS attacks—a defensive bulwark and a strategic weapon. By understanding the threats, prioritizing risks, and charting a comprehensive defensive strategy, organizations can navigate the treacherous waters of cyberspace, safeguarding their assets against the storm of DDoS attacks. In this digital age, where the threats are as dynamic as they are dangerous, this proactive and strategic approach is not just advisable; it is indispensable.

Conducting a Cybersecurity Risk Assessment

The initial stride in conducting a risk assessment involves defining the scope. It's akin to drawing a map of the territory you plan to explore, marking the boundaries, and identifying the key assets that lie within. These assets are not merely servers and databases but extend to intellectual property, customer data, and the organization's reputation—each a pillar supporting the edifice of the business.

Preparation further entails assembling a multidisciplinary team —technocrats, business unit leaders, and cybersecurity experts —each bringing a unique lens to view the organization's digital landscape. Together, they formulate the assessment's foundation, defining what success looks like and the metrics to gauge it.

With the scope delineated, the next step involves a deep dive into the organization's digital realm to catalogue and value assets. This process, meticulous by necessity, ensures every piece of hardware, every line of code, and every data byte is accounted for. The valuation isn't merely monetary but considers the asset's value to the organization's operations and its significance in the competitive landscape.

Herein lies the crux of the risk assessment—identifying the threats and vulnerabilities that could potentially compromise the identified assets. This stage is a blend of technical acumen and creative thinking, as the team deploys a suite of tools to scan for vulnerabilities and exercises scenario planning to envisage potential threat vectors, including those that could herald a DDoS attack.

Threat identification catalogues potential adversaries and their capabilities, from cybercriminals and hacktivists to state-sponsored entities. Vulnerability identification, meanwhile, employs both automated tools and manual expertise to uncover weaknesses—outdated software, misconfigured networks, and lapses in security protocols.

Armed with an inventory of assets, threats, and vulnerabilities, the assessment proceeds to risk analysis. This phase computes the likelihood of each identified risk materializing and its potential impact, should it do so. The result is a risk matrix that prioritizes risks, guiding the organization on where to focus its defensive strategies.

This quantification and prioritization hinge on both objective data and the seasoned judgement of the assessment team, ensuring that resources are allocated efficiently, safeguarding the most critical assets first.

The culmination of the risk assessment is the formulation of an action plan. This comprehensive blueprint outlines the strategies and measures to mitigate identified risks, detailing specific actions, timelines, and responsible parties. For vulnerabilities that could lead to DDoS attacks, the plan might include enhancing network resilience, implementing advanced DDoS mitigation solutions, and establishing protocols for rapid response.

The action plan is not static; it's a living document that evolves in tandem with the digital landscape. Regular reviews and updates ensure that the organization remains several steps ahead of potential adversaries, ready to adapt its defenses to emerging threats.

Conducting a cybersecurity risk assessment is a fundamental exercise in building and maintaining a resilient digital infrastructure. It enables organizations to shine a light into the darkest corners of their digital domains, identifying and addressing vulnerabilities before they can be exploited. In the ongoing battle against cyber threats, a meticulously conducted risk assessment is an indispensable tool in the arsenal of any organization serious about safeguarding its digital future against the ever-present threat of DDoS attacks and beyond.

Developing a DDOS Response Plan

Before drafting a response plan, it is vital to grasp the nature of DDoS attacks fully. These attacks, as discussed in previous sections, can vary in form and intensity, from volumetric attacks designed to overwhelm bandwidth to application-layer attacks targeting specific aspects of a service. An effective response plan begins with a thorough analysis of potential attack vectors specific to the organization's online footprint.

A dedicated response team is the linchpin of any effective DDoS response plan. This team should encompass members from various departments—IT, security, communications, and executive leadership. Each member brings a unique perspective and skill set, creating a versatile group capable of addressing the multifaceted challenges posed by DDoS attacks. The formation of this team ensures that when an attack occurs, the organization can respond swiftly and efficiently.

Early detection of a DDoS attack is critical to its mitigation. The response plan must include the implementation of monitoring tools capable of detecting abnormal traffic patterns and signs of an impending attack. These tools, coupled with a well-defined protocol for escalating alerts to the response team, form the first line of defense against DDoS assaults.

Once an attack is detected, the focus shifts to mitigation strategies. Here, the response plan outlines specific techniques tailored to the organization's network architecture and the nature of its digital assets. Strategies may include rate limiting, traffic shaping, or the deployment of web application firewalls (WAFs). Additionally, the plan should address the resilience of the infrastructure, exploring options for redundant network paths and distributed resources to dilute the impact of an attack.

Effective communication, both internal and external, is crucial during a DDoS attack. The response plan must delineate clear communication channels and responsibilities, ensuring that stakeholders are informed without causing undue alarm. External communication, particularly to customers, should be handled with care, balancing transparency with the need to protect sensitive information.

No organization is an island, particularly in the context of DDoS defense. The response plan should include protocols for engaging with external partners, including ISPs, cloud service providers, and specialized DDoS mitigation services. These relationships can be instrumental in deflecting attacks and restoring services, providing access to additional resources and expertise.

A DDoS response plan is not a static document but a living strategy that evolves in response to new threats and technological advancements. Regular reviews and updates are essential, as is the practice of conducting simulated attacks to test the plan's efficacy. These simulations, often referred to as "tabletop exercises," provide valuable insights into the plan's strengths and weaknesses, offering opportunities for continual improvement.

Developing a DDoS response plan is a comprehensive process that requires attention to detail, cross-departmental collaboration, and a proactive approach to network security. By anticipating potential attacks and preparing accordingly, an organization can protect its digital assets, maintain business continuity, and uphold its reputation in the face of this ever-evolving threat. In the digital age, a well-crafted DDoS response plan is not just a recommendation; it is a necessity for ensuring the resilience and reliability of an organization's online presence.

Importance of Regular Updates and Patches

To appreciate the importance of updates and patches, one must first understand what vulnerabilities are. In essence, vulnerabilities are flaws or weaknesses within a system that, if exploited by cyber attackers, can lead to unauthorized access, data breaches, or service disruptions. These vulnerabilities can arise from outdated software, unpatched systems, or obsolete technologies. The role of updates and patches is to address these vulnerabilities, fortifying the system against potential exploits.

Patches are corrections or modifications made to software and systems to fix known vulnerabilities. The developers of software and operating systems release patches when they discover vulnerabilities that could compromise security or functionality. By regularly applying these patches, an organization can close off avenues that attackers might use to initiate a DDoS attack or infiltrate the network.

While patches often focus on specific vulnerabilities, updates encompass broader improvements to software and systems. These may include enhancements to performance, compatibility, and security measures. Updates can also introduce new features that better meet the users' needs. In the context of DDoS defense, updates play a crucial role by ensuring that the system's security measures are aligned with the latest threats and defense strategies.

Despite the recognized importance of updates and patches, many organizations struggle with implementing them in a timely manner. This challenge can stem from various factors, including the complexity of the IT environment, the need to minimize downtime, and the potential for compatibility issues. Nevertheless, the risk of leaving systems unpatched—a veritable open door for attackers—underscores the necessity of overcoming these hurdles.

Effective patch management requires a proactive and organized approach. This includes inventorying all assets within the IT environment, prioritizing updates based on the severity of vulnerabilities, and automating the patching process where possible. Additionally, it's crucial to test patches in a controlled environment before widespread deployment to ensure they do not introduce new issues.

A comprehensive DDoS response plan recognizes the importance of regular updates and patches as a preventive measure. This plan should detail the procedures for monitoring for new patches, assessing risks, and implementing patches efficiently. Furthermore, the plan should outline the roles and responsibilities within the organization for managing updates, ensuring accountability and swift action.

The importance of regular updates and patches in the context of DDoS defense cannot be overstated. It's a testament to the fact that in the digital realm, security is not a one-time effort but a continuous process of improvement and adaptation. By fostering a culture of vigilance and prioritizing regular updates and patches, organizations can significantly enhance their resilience against DDoS attacks and other cybersecurity threats. It's a strategic investment in the reliability and integrity of the digital infrastructure that supports the modern organization's operations.

Infrastructure Design Considerations

At the core of designing a robust infrastructure lies the principle of resilience. This concept extends beyond mere resistance to attacks; it embodies the ability of a network to adapt, recover, and maintain operational continuity in the face of disruptions. Resilience in infrastructure design involves the integration of redundancy, fault tolerance, and scalable resources. It's about creating a system that can absorb the shock of a DDoS attack and continue functioning, albeit perhaps at a reduced capacity.

Redundancy is critical for ensuring that there are backup systems and components that can take over in case of failure. However, it's not as simple as duplicating every element. Strategic redundancy involves identifying critical components whose failure would cripple the network and ensuring those elements have backups. The challenge lies in balancing redundancy with cost-effectiveness, as unnecessary duplication can lead to inflated expenses without proportionate increases in security.

A network's ability to scale resources up or down based on demand is crucial in managing sudden spikes in traffic, as seen in DDoS attacks. Cloud-based services excel in this aspect, offering elasticity that can be a significant advantage during an attack. Designing an infrastructure with scalability in mind ensures that it can handle unexpected loads, providing a buffer against the flood of requests characteristic of DDoS tactics.

The inevitability of system failures demands a design philosophy that anticipates and mitigates such events without significant disruption. Fault tolerance involves the deployment of systems that can continue operating even when parts of the network fail. This approach requires a detailed analysis of potential failure points and the implementation of systems that can reroute traffic, manage data integrity, and maintain service levels even under duress.

Embracing a distributed architecture can enhance the resilience of an infrastructure against DDoS attacks. By dispersing resources across multiple locations, the impact of an attack on any single point is minimized. This distribution can be geographical, across different data centers, or even architectural, through the use of microservices. The goal is to avoid single points of failure that could render the entire network vulnerable.

Security should be an integral part of the infrastructure design process, not an afterthought. This involves the early integration of security measures, from firewalls and intrusion detection systems to encryption and access control mechanisms. By considering security at every stage of design, organizations can ensure that protective measures are woven into the fabric of their network.

Infrastructure design is not a static process; it requires regular review and adaptation to respond to evolving threats. This iterative process involves constant monitoring, analysis of attack trends, and the integration of new technologies and methodologies to counteract them. It's a cycle of continuous improvement, seeking to stay one step ahead of attackers.

Designing an infrastructure capable of defending against DDoS attacks requires meticulous planning and a deep understanding of both the threats and the tools at one's disposal. It's about crafting a digital ecosystem that prioritizes resilience, integrates security from the ground up, and remains agile in the face of evolving cyber threats. By considering these design considerations, organizations can build a network infrastructure not just to survive but to thrive, even under the relentless pressure of cyber assaults.

Designing a Resilient Network Architecture

A resilient network architecture champions the principle of a layered defense strategy, or defense in depth. This methodology employs multiple layers of security controls and measures spread throughout the network. The idea is to create a multi-faceted defense system where if one layer fails, others continue to provide protection. Incorporating firewalls, intrusion detection systems (IDS), intrusion prevention systems (IPS), and anti-DDoS solutions at different points in the network ensures that security is not reliant on a single element.

Adaptive security is a cornerstone of resilient network architecture. Dynamic segmentation subdivides the network into smaller, manageable segments, each with distinct security policies and controls. This approach not only simplifies security management but also limits the lateral movement of threats within the network. By isolating critical assets and applying stringent security measures to sensitive segments, organizations can tailor their defense mechanisms to the unique requirements of different network zones.

Visibility is the vanguard of network resilience. The implementation of comprehensive monitoring and analysis tools across the network architecture is vital. These systems provide real-time insights into network traffic, detect anomalies, and identify potential threats before they can inflict damage. Employing Security Information and Event Management (SIEM) systems and network behavior analysis tools enhances the ability to detect and respond to DDoS attacks swiftly and efficiently.

In the arms race against cyber threats, automation powered by AI and machine learning is the game-changer. Integrating these technologies into the network architecture facilitates the automation of threat detection, analysis, and response processes. AI-driven tools can analyze vast datasets to identify patterns indicative of DDoS attacks, predict potential vulnerabilities, and automatically initiate defensive actions without human intervention. This not only speeds up the response time but also alleviates the burden on cybersecurity teams.

A resilient network architecture is incomplete without robust backup and recovery strategies. These are critical in minimizing downtime and ensuring rapid restoration of services in the aftermath of an attack. Implementing redundant network paths, data backup solutions, and disaster recovery plans are essential components. Regular testing and updating of these strategies ensure they are effective when needed most.

Building a resilient network architecture is not solely a technical endeavor; it requires collaboration across various departments and integration with business processes. Security policies should align with organizational objectives, and all stakeholders must understand their roles in maintaining network resilience. Furthermore, integrating security devices and systems to enable seamless communication and data sharing enhances the overall effectiveness of the network's defense strategy.

Designing a resilient network architecture is a complex, yet critical, endeavor in safeguarding against DDoS attacks. It requires a holistic approach, combining advanced technologies, strategic planning, and a culture of continuous improvement. By embedding resilience into the very fabric of the network architecture, organizations can navigate the tumultuous waters of the digital age, not just surviving but thriving amidst the ever-evolving threat landscape. Through meticulous design and unwavering vigilance, the digital frontier can be fortified, ensuring a secure and prosperous future in the cyber realm.

The Role of Redundancy and Distributed Network Resources

redundancy in network architecture refers to the integration of additional or duplicate systems, services, or pathways that are not necessary for normal operations but are indispensable in the event of failure or attack. The principle of redundancy is predicated on the understanding that singular points of failure represent critical vulnerabilities in the network infrastructure. By implementing redundant systems—whether they be servers, data centers, connections, or even entire network paths—organizations can ensure that the failure of one component does not cascade into a systemic collapse.

The distribution of network resources across multiple, geographically dispersed locations is a strategic maneuver that significantly amplifies resilience against DDoS attacks. This decentralization strategy mitigates the risk of a single, catastrophic event compromising the entirety of an organization's digital assets and operations. Distributed networks are inherently more difficult for attackers to target effectively, as the dispersion of resources requires them to not only identify multiple targets but also to have the capacity to simultaneously overwhelm several points of defense.

Load balancing is the technological artistry that underpins both redundancy and the distribution of resources. By intelligently distributing traffic across multiple servers or data centers, load balancers ensure that no single node bears an unsustainable burden. In the context of DDoS defense, load balancing acts as a dynamic shield, dispersing potentially malicious traffic spikes across a wider surface area, thereby minimizing their impact. Advanced load balancing solutions can also discern and reroute malicious traffic away from critical assets, further enhancing network resilience.

A network designed with redundancy and distributed resources inherently possesses greater scalability. As traffic volumes grow or as the network's role within an organization expands, the ability to scale up capabilities without extensive reconfiguration or downtime becomes a significant advantage. In battling DDoS attacks, scalability allows for the rapid provisioning of additional resources to counteract large-scale threats, ensuring that defensive measures can evolve in tandem with the sophistication and scale of attacks.

Incorporating cloud-based services into the network architecture extends the principles of redundancy and resource distribution beyond the physical confines of an organization. Cloud providers typically offer highly resilient infrastructure, with built-in redundancy and distributed resources across global data centers. Leveraging cloud services for critical operations or as part of a DDoS mitigation strategy allows organizations to benefit from the scalability and advanced protection mechanisms that cloud platforms provide.

Redundancy and the strategic distribution of network resources are not merely technical considerations; they are essential strategies that imbue a network with the resilience required to withstand the onslaught of DDoS attacks. Through careful planning, implementation of load balancing, and the integration of cloud services, organizations can construct a network architecture that not only endures but also adapts and thrives in the face of cyber adversities. As the digital landscape evolves, embracing these principles is paramount in securing the future of our digital world against the ever-present threat of DDoS attacks.

Cloud Services and Their Impact on DDOS Attack Mitigation

Cloud computing, with its distributed nature, inherently

embodies the principles of redundancy and resource distribution, making it a formidable opponent against DDoS attacks. Unlike traditional on-premise infrastructures, cloud services operate across vast networks of globally dispersed data centers, each equipped with high-bandwidth capacities and sophisticated traffic filtering technologies. This unique architecture not only diffuses the risk associated with centralized resources but also provides a virtually limitless pool of bandwidth to absorb and dilute volumetric DDoS attacks.

One of the most effective weapons in the cloud's arsenal against DDoS attacks is its ability to perform advanced traffic scrubbing. This process involves the meticulous examination of incoming traffic to distinguish between legitimate users and malicious requests. Once identified, illegitimate traffic is rerouted or neutralized, ensuring that only clean traffic reaches the intended destination. Cloud providers continuously update their scrubbing technologies to adapt to evolving attack methodologies, offering a dynamic shield that evolves in lockstep with the threat landscape.

Auto-scaling, a hallmark of cloud services, allows systems to automatically adjust their resource allocation based on real-time demand. In the context of DDoS defense, auto-scaling acts as a critical countermeasure to volumetric attacks, which aim to overwhelm systems with a tsunami of traffic. By dynamically provisioning additional computing resources during an attack, cloud services can maintain operational continuity, ensuring that services remain available even under duress.

Cloud services have significantly lowered the barriers to entry for advanced DDoS mitigation strategies. Previously, only large corporations could afford the exorbitant costs associated with building and maintaining comprehensive DDoS defense mechanisms. Today, cloud providers offer these capabilities as part of their standard service offerings, enabling businesses of all sizes to benefit from high-level protection without the need for substantial upfront investments. This democratization of defense plays a crucial role in leveling the playing field, allowing smaller entities to safeguard their digital assets effectively.

Beyond the technical capabilities, cloud services act as conglomerates of collective cybersecurity intelligence. By hosting a multitude of clients, cloud providers gather vast amounts of data on emerging threats, attack patterns, and effective countermeasures. This knowledge is harnessed to fortify the defenses of all hosted entities, ensuring that each new attack enhances the collective resilience of the cloud. Furthermore, cloud providers often collaborate with cybersecurity experts and law enforcement to share threat intelligence, contributing to a broader understanding and mitigation of DDoS threats.

The integration of cloud services into DDoS mitigation strategies marks a significant evolution in cyber defense tactics. By combining the inherent advantages of cloud computing with cutting-edge technologies and collaborative intelligence, cloud services offer a robust, scalable, and cost-effective shield against DDoS attacks. As the complexity and frequency of these attacks continue to rise, the role of cloud services in cyber defense will only grow in importance, signaling a shift towards more adaptive, resilient, and democratically available cybersecurity solutions.

Exploring the multifaceted impact of cloud services on DDoS attack mitigation, we gain insight into the future of cybersecurity—a future where the agility, intelligence, and collective strength of cloud computing form the cornerstone of digital defense.

Implementing Strong Security Policies

The formulation of a security policy begins with a comprehensive risk assessment, identifying the potential vulnerabilities within an organization's digital and physical infrastructure. In the context of DDoS mitigation, this involves a meticulous analysis of network architecture, application interfaces, and data flow mechanisms to pinpoint where the organization is most susceptible to attack.

A robust security policy encompasses a broad spectrum of protocols, from employee access controls and data encryption standards to incident response strategies and recovery procedures. It articulates clear guidelines on password management, two-factor authentication, regular software updates, and the deployment of anti-DDoS measures such as traffic scrubbing and rate limiting.

The mere drafting of a security policy does not equate to protection. Enforcement is the keystone of effectiveness. This necessitates regular training sessions for employees to ensure they are acquainted with the policy's mandates and understand their personal roles in the organization's cybersecurity framework. Simulated cyberattack exercises can reinforce these concepts, providing practical experience in identifying and responding to potential threats.

Moreover, the enforcement of security policies requires the establishment of a dedicated oversight body within the organization. This team is tasked with monitoring compliance, conducting periodic audits, and updating the policy in alignment with emerging cyber threats and evolving industry best practices.

Technology plays a pivotal role in ensuring the consistent application of security policies across an organization's digital domain. Automated tools can monitor network traffic in real-time, flagging anomalies that may indicate a DDoS attack in progress. Similarly, automated patch management systems can ensure that all software is up-to-date, closing vulnerabilities that could be exploited by attackers.

In the realm of access control, identity and access management (IAM) solutions can enforce strict adherence to security policies, ensuring that only authorized personnel can access sensitive information and systems. These technological guardrails are indispensable allies in the quest for policy compliance.

The cyber threat landscape is in constant flux, with attackers continually devising new methodologies to breach defenses. As such, security policies cannot remain static. They must evolve in tandem with the threat environment, incorporating lessons learned from recent attacks and integrating advancements in cybersecurity technology.

This requires a commitment to ongoing education and vigilance, with organizations staying abreast of the latest cybersecurity research, attending industry conferences, and participating in professional forums. By fostering a culture of continuous improvement and adaptation, businesses can ensure that their security policies remain an effective shield against DDoS attacks and other cyber threats.

Implementing strong security policies is not a one-time endeavor but a continuous journey toward cyber resilience. Through the careful development, rigorous enforcement, technological augmentation, and dynamic evolution of these policies, organizations can fortify their defenses against the ever-present threat of DDoS attacks. In the digital age, a well-crafted security policy is not just a document—it is the very bedrock upon which the security of the organization rests, providing a framework for proactive defense and strategic response in the face of an ever-changing cyber threat landscape.

Development and Enforcement of Comprehensive Security Policies

The initiation of a security policy is predicated upon an astute understanding of the organization's unique ecosystem – its technological infrastructure, data flows, human elements, and the potential cyber threat vectors it faces. This nuanced comprehension allows for the tailoring of policies that are as much about prevention as they are about response. In the specific context of DDoS defense, the policy must detail preventive measures such as the deployment of web application firewalls (WAFs) and DDoS mitigation services, alongside response strategies that delineate steps to be taken in the event of an attack.

A comprehensive policy is also inclusive of guidelines on secure code development practices, defining standards that minimize vulnerabilities in software from the outset. Additionally, it addresses the human factor – specifying training programs on phishing attack recognition and secure password practices, thereby fortifying the organization's first line of defense.

The greatest challenge in cybersecurity is not the formulation of policies but their enforcement and adherence. A dynamic approach to enforcement involves not just disciplinary measures for non-compliance but also a system of rewards that recognize and incentivize adherence. Regular, unannounced cybersecurity drills can test the organization's readiness, while cybersecurity audits – both internal and external – assess the compliance level and efficacy of the enforcement mechanisms in place.

Crucially, enforcement is not the purview of the IT department alone but a shared responsibility across the organization. This necessitates the designation of cybersecurity champions within various departments, who act as liaisons with the IT security team and ensure that the security policies are understood and implemented within their respective domains.

In the age of sophisticated cyber threats, leveraging technology for policy enforcement is not an option but a necessity. Automated systems can provide real-time alerts on security breaches or policy violations, enabling swift action. Artificial Intelligence (AI) and Machine Learning (ML) algorithms can predict potential threat patterns and automate responses, thus augmenting the human effort in cybersecurity.

Moreover, Secure Access Service Edge (SASE) and Zero Trust architectures can enforce policy compliance by design, ensuring that access to resources is strictly based on the principle of least privilege and continuously verified, thus significantly mitigating the risk of DDoS and other cyber-attacks.

In the digital landscape, where change is the only constant, security policies cannot afford to be static. They must evolve in response to new threats, technological advancements, and lessons learned from past incidents. This requires a feedback loop where insights from attack analyses, technological trends, and employee feedback inform regular policy updates. Such a living document not only stays relevant but also reinforces the organization's commitment to a culture of continuous improvement in cybersecurity.

The development and vigorous enforcement of comprehensive security policies are paramount in safeguarding an organization against the relentless barrage of cyber threats, especially DDoS attacks. This endeavor, while challenging, is indispensable for cultivating an environment of cyber resilience. By meticulously crafting, enforcing, and refining these policies, organizations can wield them not merely as shields against threats but as strategic assets that foster trust, innovation, and growth in the digital age.

Employee Training and Awareness Programs

The journey towards a cyber-resilient organization begins with the crafting of a comprehensive curriculum that addresses the full spectrum of cyber threats, with particular emphasis on the mechanics, recognition, and prevention of DDoS attacks. This curriculum should be tailored to the varied levels of technical proficiency within the organization, ensuring accessibility and comprehension for all employees.

Interactive modules that simulate phishing attempts, password cracking, and even the staging of a mock DDoS attack can dramatically enhance engagement and retention of information. Such hands-on experiences demystify cyber threats and empower employees with the confidence to act decisively in real-world scenarios.

Cyber threats evolve with dizzying speed, rendering once-vigilant defenses obsolete. In this context, training and awareness programs cannot be a one-off event but must be embedded into the fabric of the organization's culture as a continuous learning process. Regular updates to the training material, in response to emerging threats and technologies, ensure that the organization's defenses remain robust and responsive.

Incorporating cybersecurity topics into regular team meetings, creating a dedicated intranet site with resources and updates, and encouraging participation in external webinars and courses are strategies that can foster an environment of ongoing education and vigilance.

The effectiveness of training and awareness programs is contingent upon their ability to engage employees and instill actionable knowledge. Regular testing, through quizzes, practical exercises, and cyber wargaming exercises, serves as both a reinforcement tool and a metric for engagement and comprehension.

Feedback mechanisms where employees can share their experiences, suggest improvements, and even contribute to the training content can enhance the program's relevance and efficacy. Recognition and rewards for cybersecurity champions who demonstrate exceptional vigilance or improvement can further incentivize engagement.

While general training serves the broader purpose of creating a baseline of cyber awareness, specialized training for IT staff, particularly those involved in network and security operations, is crucial. These programs should delve deeper into the technical aspects of DDoS defense mechanisms, covering advanced topics such as traffic analysis, intrusion detection systems, and the intricacies of DDoS mitigation technologies.

Collaboration with external experts, participation in industry conferences, and certification programs can ensure that the IT team remains at the cutting edge of cybersecurity practices, capable of defending the organization's digital assets against sophisticated attacks.

Where the human factor often represents the weakest link in the cybersecurity chain, employee training and awareness programs stand as the first line of defense. By fostering a culture of cyber literacy and vigilance, organizations can transform their employees from potential vulnerabilities into robust human firewalls. These programs, when executed with commitment and creativity, not only protect against the immediate threat of DDoS attacks but also contribute to the formation of a resilient, informed, and proactive cyber workforce.

Regular Security Audits and the Role of Penetration Testing

Security audits serve as a comprehensive evaluation of an organization's adherence to cybersecurity policies and standards. These audits, akin to a detailed map of the fortress's defenses, provide a holistic view of the organization's cyber health, identifying strengths and exposing vulnerabilities that could be exploited in a DDoS attack or other cyber intrusions.

The process should be both rigorous and recurring, encompassing a review of physical security measures, network and application vulnerability assessments, and an examination of operative procedures and employee compliance. The outcome of these audits should result in actionable insights, guiding the fortification of defenses and the remediation of identified weaknesses.

Penetration testing, or pen testing, complements security audits by simulating cyber-attacks on an organization's systems to evaluate the effectiveness of its security measures. This practice is the crucible in which the theoretical defenses erected by the organization are tested against the cunning and creativity of real-world cyber threats.

Pen testers, operating as benevolent hackers, employ a myriad of techniques – from IP spoofing, which is often used in DDoS attacks, to social engineering and beyond. Their objective is to identify any breachable points in the organization's cyber armor. The insights gleaned from these exercises are invaluable, offering a direct line of sight into potential vulnerabilities and the effectiveness of the organization's incident response protocols.

The integration of regular security audits and penetration testing into the cybersecurity strategy is not merely a tactical choice but a strategic necessity. This dual approach ensures that the organization's defenses are not only theoretically sound but have been battle-tested against the ingenuity of simulated cyber assaults.

To operationalize this strategy, organizations must adopt a cycle of continuous improvement, where the findings from audits and pen tests inform the ongoing refinement of security policies, the hardening of systems, and the training of personnel. This cycle, characterized by assessment, adaptation, and re-assessment, is foundational to maintaining a posture of resilience in the face of an ever-evolving threat landscape.

In the context of DDoS defense, regular audits should include a specific focus on the organization's capacity to detect, mitigate, and recover from such attacks. This includes the evaluation of network bandwidth, the robustness of server infrastructure, and the effectiveness of DDoS mitigation services and software.

Penetration testing should similarly be tailored to simulate DDoS scenarios, assessing the organization's response mechanisms and the latency in activating defensive protocols. This specialized focus ensures that preparations are not just theoretical but are calibrated against the practical realities of DDoS warfare.

The implementation of regular security audits and penetration testing cultivates a culture of proactive defense, where cybersecurity is understood as a dynamic, integral component of the organization's operational rhythm. This approach not only enhances the organization's resilience against DDoS attacks and other cyber threats but also embeds cybersecurity as a cornerstone of organizational integrity, ensuring the protection of data, assets, and reputation in the digital era.

CHAPTER 5: ADVANCED PROTECTIVE MEASURES

B GP, is a protocol used by Internet routers to exchange routing information between autonomous systems (AS), which are collections of IP networks and routers under the control of one or more network operators that present a common routing policy to the internet. Despite its critical role in the functionality of the internet, BGP was designed in an era where trust was implicit, which has led to significant security challenges.

The foundational issue with BGP lies in its trust-based model, where announcements from AS to AS are accepted without verification. This has led to several types of attacks, including:

1. Prefix Hijacking: Where an AS maliciously or erroneously announces ownership of IP address blocks that it does not actually control. This can lead to traffic meant for one destination being diverted to another, potentially malicious,

destination.

2. AS Path Manipulation: By altering the AS path information in a BGP announcement, an attacker can reroute traffic through their AS, enabling them to eavesdrop or perform man-in-the-middle attacks.

3. Route Flapping: Frequent, rapid announcements and withdrawals of routes cause instability and can overload routers, leading to denial of service.

These vulnerabilities not only compromise the security of data transmission but also the stability and reliability of internet connectivity.

Mitigating the risks associated with BGP requires a multifaceted approach, incorporating both operational practices and technical solutions:

1. Route Filtering: Network operators can implement route filtering to only allow BGP announcements that are expected and legitimate based on known information, such as the expected IP addresses and AS paths.

2. BGP Route Origin Validation: Solutions like the Resource Public Key Infrastructure (RPKI) enable the validation of route origins, allowing routers to verify that a BGP announcement is being made by the actual owner of the IP address block. This significantly reduces the risk of prefix hijacking.

3. BGPsec: An extension of BGP, BGPsec provides a means to validate the entire AS path, ensuring that the path has not been tampered with. By leveraging cryptographic signatures, BGPsec

adds a layer of security that makes it much harder for attackers to manipulate routing information maliciously.

In the context of Distributed Denial of Service (DDoS) defense, BGP plays a pivotal role. By controlling routing paths, BGP can be leveraged to reroute traffic through scrubbing centers or other mitigation services designed to cleanse the traffic of malicious packets before forwarding it to its intended destination. This capability makes BGP a critical tool in the arsenal against large-scale DDoS attacks, which seek to overwhelm network resources.

However, the effectiveness of BGP in this role is contingent upon the robustness of its security. A compromised BGP can, conversely, be used to exacerbate a DDoS attack by redirecting additional malicious traffic towards the target or by inhibiting the rerouting of traffic to mitigation services.

The security of BGP is foundational to the security and reliability of the internet. As cyber threats evolve, the methodologies for securing BGP must also advance. Through the implementation of technical solutions such as RPKI and BGPsec, alongside rigorous operational practices, we can safeguard this critical infrastructure from exploitation. The ongoing efforts to enhance BGP security not only protect against traditional threats but also fortify defenses against complex cyber-attacks such as DDoS, ensuring the continuity and integrity of global internet connectivity.

Understanding BGP and Its Vulnerabilities

BGP functions by enabling data packets to be routed between autonomous systems (AS), which are vast collections of connected internet routes under the control of single entities or administrations. Each AS exchanges routing information with other AS through BGP, thereby determining the most efficient pathway for data packet travel. While this system is crucial for the internet's operability, it harbors significant security flaws inherited from its trust-based design.

1. Lack of Inherent Authentication:

BGP was not designed with robust security measures. The protocol inherently trusts the routing information it receives, without any form of verification. This trust model makes BGP susceptible to various types of misinformation attacks.

2. Route Hijacking:

One of the most prevalent BGP vulnerabilities is route hijacking, where an AS falsely claims ownership of an IP address block. This can divert internet traffic through the malicious AS, enabling data interception or the creation of internet black holes where data is simply dropped.

3. Route Leaks:

Route leaks occur when routing announcements extend beyond their intended scope. An AS accidentally or maliciously forwards routing announcements to AS that shouldn't receive them, causing misdirection of traffic that can lead to congestion, bottlenecks, or unintentional data interception.

4. AS Path Manipulation:

Attackers may manipulate the AS path attribute in routing announcements to reroute traffic through malicious networks. This can facilitate eavesdropping and man-in-the-middle attacks, compromising the confidentiality and integrity of the data.

5. Prefix Deaggregation:

An attacker might deaggregate IP prefixes into smaller blocks, making the routing table unnecessarily large and complex. This can overwhelm routers, leading to degraded network performance or denial of service.

The vulnerabilities in BGP are not just theoretical risks; they have tangible impacts on the real world. From causing outages of major internet platforms to enabling state-sponsored cyber espionage, the exploitation of BGP's flaws has far-reaching consequences. It affects not only the confidentiality and integrity of data but also the availability of internet services, highlighting the need for effective security measures.

In light of these vulnerabilities, the cybersecurity community has endeavored to develop solutions such as Route Origin Authorizations (ROAs) with the Resource Public Key Infrastructure (RPKI) for route origin validation, and BGPsec for path validation. However, the implementation of these solutions is uneven across the global internet, partly due to their operational complexity and the need for widespread cooperation among AS operators.

Understanding BGP and its vulnerabilities is crucial for cybersecurity professionals and network operators alike. As the lifeline of the internet, securing BGP against potential threats is imperative to ensure the stability and reliability of global internet infrastructure. Through collective efforts in implementing security best practices, adopting advanced security protocols, and fostering a culture of vigilance and cooperation, the internet community can shield BGP from exploitation and fortify the digital ecosystem against disruptions.

Techniques for Securing BGP: Route Filtering and RPKI

Route Filtering represents a fundamental approach to enhancing BGP security, predicated on the meticulous scrutiny of routing information. This technique involves the establishment of policies that precisely define which routes are valid and thereby should be accepted or propagated. Route Filtering acts as a gatekeeper, scrutinizing each routing update based on predefined criteria, thus preventing the propagation of erroneous or malicious routes.

Implementing Route Filtering:

- Prefix Lists: Administrators can deploy prefix lists to specify allowable prefixes that an AS can advertise, effectively blocking unauthorized route announcements.

- AS Path Filters: These filters scrutinize the AS path attribute of BGP routes, allowing only routes that traverse through trusted ASes, thereby mitigating the risk of AS path manipulation.

- Community Attribute Filters: Leveraging BGP community attributes enables the categorization of routes. Policies can then permit or deny routing updates based on these categories, offering a granular level of control.

While Route Filtering provides a robust first line of defense, the Resource Public Key Infrastructure (RPKI) introduces an additional layer of security by anchoring BGP route authenticity in cryptographic verification. RPKI is a framework designed to secure the internet's routing infrastructure by enabling the association of internet resources (e.g., IP addresses and AS numbers) with a digital certificate, verifying the rightful ownership and legitimacy of these resources.

Core Aspects of RPKI:

- Route Origin Authorizations (ROAs): At the heart of RPKI are ROAs, which are essentially digital certificates that validate that a specific AS is authorized to announce a particular IP address prefix. ROAs serve as proof of legitimacy, curtailing the ability of malicious actors to hijack routes.

- RPKI Validators: These are tools that download and verify the authenticity of RPKI data from trusted repositories. Validators make this information available to routers, which can then make informed decisions on whether to accept or reject a route based on its validation status.

Deploying RPKI:

Implementing RPKI necessitates cooperation among all stakeholders in the internet ecosystem. Network operators must create ROAs for their internet resources, and AS operators need to configure their routers to perform RPKI validation. Despite its effectiveness, the adoption of RPKI has been gradual, underscoring the need for increased awareness and capacity-building efforts within the community.

Combining Route Filtering with RPKI offers a synergistic approach to securing BGP. Route Filtering provides immediate, policy-based control over routing decisions, while RPKI introduces cryptographic verification of route legitimacy.

Together, they form a comprehensive defense mechanism, significantly bolstering the resilience of the internet's routing infrastructure against attacks.

Securing BGP, the backbone of the internet's routing system, is paramount in the quest for a stable and secure cyberspace. Techniques such as Route Filtering and RPKI are instrumental in this endeavor, offering robust defenses against the exploitation of BGP's inherent vulnerabilities. By adopting these techniques, network operators can significantly enhance the security and integrity of BGP routing, contributing to the overall resilience of the internet infrastructure. Through collective and concerted efforts towards implementing these security measures, the digital community can safeguard the internet against disruptions, ensuring its continued growth and vitality in the interconnected world.

In the digital fortress that guards against the relentless onslaught of DDoS attacks, the Border Gateway Protocol (BGP) stands not only as the scaffolding of the internet's architecture but also as a strategic bulwark in defense strategies. While primarily serving as the postal service of the internet, directing data packets between autonomous systems (AS), BGP, when adeptly configured and fortified, can play a pivotal role in mitigating the impact of DDoS attacks.

One of the fundamental strategies involves the use of BGP to perform traffic engineering. By manipulating route announcements, network administrators can redirect incoming traffic across multiple pathways, preventing any single pathway from becoming overwhelmed. This approach relies on the dynamic nature of BGP to adjust routes in real-time, ensuring optimal distribution of traffic and enhancing the resilience of networks against DDoS attacks.

BGP Flowspec emerges as a formidable tool in the arsenal against DDoS attacks, enabling the quick dissemination of filtering rules across the network. By specifying traffic patterns that are indicative of a DDoS attack, BGP Flowspec allows for the immediate and automatic blocking or rate-limiting of such malicious traffic at the network's edge, curtailing its spread and impact.

RTBH filtering stands as a testament to the adaptability of BGP in the face of cyber threats. This technique involves the use of BGP to route identified malicious traffic towards a "black hole," where it is summarily dropped, preventing it from reaching its intended target. While this method is effective in shielding the target from the attack, it requires careful implementation to avoid inadvertently discarding legitimate traffic.

The battle against DDoS attacks is not fought by lone entities but through the concerted efforts of the global internet community. BGP facilitates this collaboration through the use of community tags, which can communicate information about suspicious traffic across different ASes. This shared intelligence enables a collective response to emerging threats, enhancing the capacity to mitigate DDoS attacks on a broader scale.

While BGP offers promising avenues for DDoS mitigation, it is not without its challenges. The protocol's inherent trust-based system can be exploited by attackers to introduce false routes, turning BGP itself into a vector for attack. Thus, the security of BGP, through mechanisms like RPKI and route filtering, is paramount to its effectiveness in DDoS mitigation.

Furthermore, the deployment of BGP-based DDoS mitigation techniques requires a delicate balance. Overly aggressive routing changes can disrupt normal traffic, potentially causing collateral damage. Thus, the implementation of these strategies necessitates a nuanced understanding of network dynamics and the potential implications of routing adjustments.

The role of BGP in mitigating DDoS attacks embodies the principle of adaptability in cybersecurity. By leveraging BGP's capabilities for traffic engineering, rapid response through Flowspec, RTBH filtering, and collaborative efforts, network operators can erect more resilient defenses against the scourge of DDoS attacks. However, this endeavor is not without its complexities and requires a vigilant and informed approach to maximize efficacy while minimizing unintended consequences. As the digital landscape evolves, so too must our strategies for protecting it, with BGP serving as both a tool and a testament to this ongoing battle.

In the labyrinth of the internet, the Domain Name System (DNS) acts as the compass and map, translating human-friendly domain names into IP addresses that computers use to identify each other. However, just as a map can lead treasure hunters to gold, the DNS can lead cybercriminals to their targets. Its pivotal role in the digital ecosystem makes it a prime target for DDoS attacks, necessitating robust security measures to safeguard this essential service.

DNS services are the bedrock of internet accessibility. When DNS services falter under a DDoS attack, it's akin to ripping the map from the hands of internet users—services become unreachable, websites disappear, and the seamless connectivity we take for granted crumbles. Securing DNS services, therefore, is not merely a technical necessity but a foundational aspect of maintaining the internet's usability and reliability.

The first step in securing DNS services is recognizing their vulnerabilities. DNS was designed in a more trusting internet era, and its open and distributed nature, while a strength, also presents opportunities for exploitation. DDoS attacks, such as DNS amplification, exploit these vulnerabilities, turning the DNS service itself into a weapon against other targets.

- Implementation of DNSSEC: DNS Security Extensions (DNSSEC) add a layer of security by enabling DNS responses to be authenticated. It's akin to sealing maps in tamper-evident packaging—users can be confident that the DNS information they receive has not been tampered with en route.

- Rate Limiting: Implementing rate limiting for DNS responses helps mitigate the risk of DNS amplification attacks. By controlling the flow of information, it prevents attackers from overwhelming targets with massive volumes of data.

- Diverse Service Providers: Utilizing multiple DNS service providers can offer redundancy and mitigate the risk of DDoS attacks. If one service becomes a target, others can continue to provide resolution services, ensuring uninterrupted access.

The cloud offers a resilient platform for DNS services, capable of absorbing and dispersing the traffic typical of DDoS attacks. Cloud-based DNS providers often have extensive infrastructure and sophisticated defenses specifically designed to mitigate such attacks. Moreover, these providers typically offer advanced security features, such as automated threat detection and response capabilities, further protecting DNS services from attack.

When considering cloud-based DNS services, it's crucial to

evaluate their security features, infrastructure resilience, and the ability to scale in response to attacks. The choice of provider should align with the organization's security needs and the criticality of the services reliant on DNS.

Securing DNS services extends beyond technical measures to encompass the human element. Regular training for IT staff on the latest DNS threats and mitigation strategies is essential. Vigilance, in the form of continuous monitoring of DNS traffic for signs of malicious activity, ensures that threats can be identified and addressed promptly.

Securing DNS services is a multi-faceted endeavor that requires a blend of technical solutions, strategic choices, and continuous vigilance. As gatekeepers of the internet's mapping system, DNS services demand robust protection to prevent their exploitation in DDoS attacks. By adopting best practices for DNS security, leveraging cloud-based solutions, and fostering a culture of security awareness, organizations can defend against the threats that target this critical infrastructure, ensuring that the digital compass guiding internet traffic remains accurate and secure.

DNS security is paramount because it stands at the crossroads of nearly all internet communications. An attack on DNS can misdirect users to fraudulent sites designed to steal sensitive information, distribute malware, or engage in phishing attacks. Therefore, securing DNS is akin to placing a guard at every junction in the digital world, ensuring that users reach their intended destinations safely. The trust users place in the internet's ability to connect them accurately and securely to services hinges on the robustness of DNS security measures.

A compromised DNS service doesn't just affect a single user or website; it has the potential to disrupt operations on a global scale. For instance, a DNS DDoS attack can make a multitude of websites inaccessible, impacting economies and eroding trust in digital systems. The interconnectedness of digital services means a breach in DNS security can have cascading effects, paralyzing critical infrastructure and services that rely on the internet.

As cyber threats become more sophisticated, the methods used to attack DNS infrastructure have also evolved, from straightforward DDoS attacks to more insidious forms like DNS hijacking and Cache Poisoning. These advancements make it imperative for security measures to evolve in tandem, adopting proactive and adaptive strategies to safeguard DNS services.

- Holistic Security Posture: Organizations must adopt a comprehensive security posture that includes regular audits of DNS security practices, adherence to best practices such as DNSSEC, and the implementation of redundant DNS services to ensure availability even under attack.

- Public and Private Collaboration: Strengthening DNS security is not just the responsibility of individual organizations but requires collaboration across the public and private sectors. Sharing threat intelligence and best practices can help preempt attacks and bolster collective defenses.

- Continuous Education and Awareness: Given the critical role DNS plays in the internet ecosystem, continuous education on its security challenges and best practices is essential. Organizations should prioritize training for their staff and promote awareness about DNS security in their communities.

The importance of DNS security cannot be overstated. It is

the foundation upon which the trust and reliability of the internet are built. In the digital age, where connectivity is a critical aspect of everyday life, ensuring the security of DNS services is paramount. By adopting a multifaceted approach to DNS security, involving technological solutions, collaborative efforts, and continuous education, we can safeguard the integrity of internet communications and protect against the far-reaching consequences of DNS-based attacks. The resilience of the digital world depends on our collective commitment to these principles, ensuring a secure and trustworthy internet for future generations.

Best Practices for Securing DNS: DNSSEC and Rate Limiting

DNSSEC stands as a fortress designed to protect against one of the most prevalent forms of cyber assaults - DNS spoofing. This form of attack, where the attacker diverts users to malicious websites by manipulating DNS data, can be effectively neutralized through DNSSEC.

Key Features of DNSSEC:

- Data Integrity Verification: DNSSEC ensures that the data received from a DNS query is authentic and has not been tampered with. It employs a suite of digital signatures and public-key cryptography to validate the authenticity of the data, thus safeguarding users from malicious redirects.

- Non-Repudiation: The digital signatures in DNSSEC provide a mechanism for source validation, ensuring that the data originates from a legitimate source. This feature is crucial for establishing trust in internet communications.

Implementing DNSSEC requires meticulous planning and

execution. The process involves generating cryptographic keys, signing DNS records, and publishing these in the DNS. Despite its complexity, the deployment of DNSSEC is a critical step towards a secure and resilient DNS infrastructure.

Rate limiting serves as an effective measure to mitigate Distributed Denial of Service (DDoS) attacks, which overwhelm servers with excessive requests. By imposing a limit on the number of requests a user can make within a specific timeframe, rate limiting can prevent attackers from inundating the DNS server with traffic, thus maintaining service availability even under duress.

Effective Strategies for Rate Limiting:

- Dynamic Thresholds: Setting static rate limits might not be practical due to the variability in legitimate traffic patterns. Implementing dynamic thresholds that adjust based on real-time traffic analysis can provide more flexibility and prevent legitimate requests from being blocked.

- Geographic Considerations: Attackers often utilize botnets distributed across different regions to launch their attacks. Incorporating geographic data into rate limiting decisions can help in identifying and mitigating such distributed threats more effectively.

- User Behavior Analysis: Incorporating user behavior analytics into rate limiting mechanisms can enhance the effectiveness of identifying and mitigating malicious traffic. By understanding normal user patterns, deviations that signify potential attacks can be flagged for further action.

Securing DNS is not a one-time task but a continuous

process that evolves with the threat landscape. Implementing DNSSEC and rate limiting are foundational practices that play a significant role in enhancing DNS security. DNSSEC safeguards against data manipulation, ensuring that users are not misdirected to fraudulent sites, while rate limiting serves as a critical defense mechanism against DDoS attacks. Together, these practices form a robust defense strategy, fortifying DNS infrastructure against a wide array of cyber threats. As we venture further into the digital era, the security of DNS will remain paramount in preserving the integrity and reliability of internet services, necessitating ongoing vigilance and adaptation to emerging cybersecurity challenges.

Mitigation Strategies for DNS Amplification Attacks

To effectively counter DNS amplification attacks, it's crucial to grasp their operational mechanics. These attacks involve the exploitation of publicly accessible DNS servers to flood a target with a deluge of responses. By making a small query with a spoofed IP address (that of the victim), the attacker tricks the DNS server into sending a large response to the victim's address, thereby amplifying the traffic volume exponentially.

Restricting DNS Recursion: One pivotal step in preempting DNS amplification is to limit DNS recursion. By configuring DNS servers to resolve requests only from within a trusted domain, administrators can significantly reduce the server's utility for attackers. This restriction ensures that only legitimate client requests are processed.

Rate Limiting DNS Responses: Extending the concept of rate limiting, specifically tailoring it to DNS responses can thwart amplification efforts. Implementing rate limits on DNS reply sizes and the number of responses sent per second can stifle an attack's efficacy, reducing the potential damage.

Implement DNS Response Rate Limiting (DNS RRL): DNS RRL is an effective strategy for mitigating amplification. By limiting the rate of identical responses sent from a DNS server, DNS RRL can prevent the server from being exploited as an unwitting participant in an attack.

Deploying Anomaly Detection Systems: The sudden surge in traffic volume characteristic of amplification attacks can be detected by anomaly-based intrusion detection systems. These systems, trained to recognize normal traffic patterns, can trigger alerts when deviations occur, enabling timely responses to mitigate the attack.

Utilizing Traffic Shaping: Traffic shaping, or the controlled regulation of network data transfer, can help manage the influx of amplified DNS responses. By prioritizing legitimate traffic and throttling suspicious high-volume flows, organizations can maintain operational continuity during an attack.

Employing Geo-IP Filtering: Given that attacks often originate from regions outside the victim's typical traffic patterns, implementing geo-IP filtering can block incoming requests from suspect locations. This approach requires a nuanced understanding of normal traffic sources to avoid inadvertently blocking legitimate users.

Engaging with Upstream Providers: Collaboration with internet service providers (ISPs) and other upstream entities is crucial. These partners can implement filtering and rate-limiting measures that minimize the attack traffic before it reaches the victim's network.

Participation in Threat Intelligence Sharing Platforms: Sharing information about ongoing attacks with a broader community can help in preemptively protecting against similar threats. Participation in threat intelligence networks allows for the pooling of resources and knowledge, enhancing the collective defense posture against DNS amplification attacks.

Mitigating DNS amplification attacks demands a proactive and layered security strategy. By securing DNS servers against misuse, implementing real-time detection and mitigation techniques, and engaging in collaborative defense efforts, organizations can significantly reduce their vulnerability to these disruptive attacks. The dynamic nature of cyber threats necessitates constant vigilance and adaptation of security measures to protect the integrity of network infrastructures against the evolving tactics of attackers.

Leveraging Cloud-Based DDoS Protection

Cloud-based DDoS protection operates on the principle of distributed risk mitigation. Unlike traditional on-premises solutions that rely on finite resources, cloud services can dynamically allocate vast computing resources to absorb and neutralize DDoS traffic. This process typically involves rerouting inbound traffic through the cloud provider's scrubbing centers, where malicious packets are filtered out, ensuring that only legitimate traffic reaches the target's infrastructure.

Dynamic Scalability: One of the hallmark features of cloud-based DDoS protection is its ability to scale resources on demand. During a DDoS attack, the cloud infrastructure can instantly expand its bandwidth capacity to absorb the increased traffic, a feat unattainable for most on-premise solutions without significant investment.

Distributed Protection Architecture: Cloud services employ a globally distributed network of data centers. This geographical dispersion ensures that DDoS attack traffic can be intercepted and mitigated closer to its source, reducing latency and the load on the target's network.

Cost-Effectiveness: By leveraging the cloud, organizations can benefit from high-level DDoS protection without the need for substantial capital expenditure on hardware and infrastructure. The operational expense model of cloud services allows for cost predictability and savings.

Enhanced Uptime and Availability: Cloud providers specialize in ensuring the availability of services. Their DDoS mitigation capabilities are designed to ensure that an organization's online presence remains uninterrupted, even under the duress of an ongoing attack.

Expertise and Continuous Updates: Cloud-service providers are manned by cybersecurity experts who continuously monitor emerging DDoS trends and tactics. Consequently, cloud-based DDoS protection services are regularly updated to counter new threats, offering a level of expertise and responsiveness that would be challenging to replicate in-house.

Choosing the Right Provider: Selecting a cloud provider for DDoS protection involves evaluating their service level agreements (SLAs), mitigation capacity, and the sophistication of their detection and filtering technology. It's crucial to partner with a provider that aligns with the organization's specific needs and risk profile.

Integration with Existing Security Posture: Organizations must consider how cloud-based DDoS protection will integrate with their existing security infrastructure. Seamless integration enhances the overall security posture, while disjointed systems can create gaps that attackers might exploit.

Compliance and Data Privacy: When routing traffic through cloud-based scrubbing centers, data sovereignty and privacy become paramount concerns. Organizations must ensure that their cloud-based DDoS protection strategy complies with relevant regulations and standards.

In the escalating arms race of cybersecurity, cloud-based DDoS protection emerges as a potent deterrent against the ever-evolving threat of DDoS attacks. Its scalability, cost-effectiveness, and access to expert resources offer a strategic advantage in safeguarding digital assets. However, the decision to adopt cloud-based DDoS protection must be informed by a comprehensive assessment of the organization's specific needs, risk tolerance, and compliance requirements. As cyber threats continue to proliferate, leveraging cloud-based defenses will be pivotal in fortifying the digital bastions of the future.

Pros and Cons of Cloud-Based DDoS Protection Services

1. Elastic Scalability: The cloud inherently possesses the ability to scale resources dynamically. In the context of DDoS protection, this means the capability to absorb and mitigate large-scale attack traffic that would overwhelm traditional on-premises defenses. This scalability ensures that services remain available, even under the assault of complex, high-volume DDoS attacks.

2. Cost Efficiency: Implementing and maintaining on-premises DDoS mitigation infrastructure necessitates significant upfront and ongoing investments. Cloud-based services, on the other hand, typically operate on a subscription model, which significantly reduces capital expenditure and shifts costs to a more manageable operational expense.

3. Expert Management and Up-to-Date Protection: Cloud providers specialize in security. They employ teams of experts who continuously monitor the threat landscape, update protection mechanisms, and are on standby to mitigate attacks. This level of expertise and responsiveness is challenging for individual organizations to replicate.

4. Global Threat Intelligence: Leading cloud-based DDoS protection providers aggregate data on cyber threats from across their global customer base. This intelligence allows them to identify and mitigate new DDoS attack vectors swiftly, offering a level of proactive protection that benefits all their clients.

1. Potential for Latency: Routing traffic through a cloud provider's scrubbing centers can introduce latency. While this is often minimal, for latency-sensitive applications, even a slight delay can impact performance. It's crucial for organizations to assess the latency implications of their chosen cloud-based DDoS protection service.

2. Data Privacy Concerns: Utilizing cloud-based services necessitates sending traffic outside the organization's direct control, raising concerns about data privacy and compliance, particularly for businesses governed by strict regulatory requirements.

3. Dependency on Internet Connectivity: Cloud-based DDoS protection is inherently reliant on internet connectivity. Should an organization's internet connection be disrupted, the protective benefits of the cloud service are nullified, leaving the organization's assets vulnerable.

4. False Positives and Negatives: No DDoS protection service is infallible. False positives, where legitimate traffic is mistakenly identified as malicious, can block access to genuine users. Conversely, false negatives may allow some attack traffic through. Balancing sensitivity to effectively mitigate attacks while minimizing false positives is a complex challenge.

Deciding whether to adopt cloud-based DDoS protection services requires a careful assessment of an organization's specific needs, existing security infrastructure, regulatory landscape, and risk tolerance. The decision should involve a comprehensive analysis of the service provider's capabilities, including their mitigation capacity, response times, and the geographical distribution of their scrubbing centers.

For organizations whose operations are heavily dependent on online presence and services, the advantages of cloud-based DDoS protection—particularly its scalability and expert management—often outweigh the limitations. Nonetheless, it's crucial for businesses to conduct due diligence, potentially seeking trials or pilot programs, to ensure the chosen solution aligns with their operational requirements and security posture.

while cloud-based DDoS protection services present an effective means to counteract the growing menace of DDoS attacks, organizations must embark on this path with a clear understanding of both the benefits and the trade-offs. A strategic approach, one that considers the organization's unique context and the evolving cyber threat landscape, will be key to harnessing the full potential of cloud-based defenses in the quest for cyber resilience.

How Cloud Services Can Absorb and Mitigate DDoS Attacks

At the heart of cloud-based DDoS mitigation is the concept of absorption capacity. Cloud platforms, with their vast networks of globally distributed servers, possess an inherent ability to absorb volumetric attack traffic that would easily overwhelm the bandwidth of most standalone websites or corporate networks. This capacity is not merely a function of size but also of the cloud's dynamic scalability. Cloud services can automatically allocate more resources in response to increased demand, whether from legitimate users or an attack, ensuring that traffic continues to flow and services remain online.

Beyond mere absorption, the efficacy of cloud services in mitigating DDoS attacks lies in their sophisticated traffic analysis capabilities. Utilizing advanced algorithms and machine learning models, these services scrutinize incoming traffic patterns in real-time, identifying and filtering out malicious packets while allowing legitimate traffic to pass. This process involves examining various attributes of the traffic, such as IP addresses, packet types, and behavior patterns, to detect and neutralize potential threats before they reach the target server.

Cloud services deploy a repertoire of techniques to combat DDoS attacks, each tailored to neutralize specific attack vectors:

- Rate Limiting: By monitoring and controlling the rate of requests a server handles, cloud services can prevent the server from becoming overwhelmed. This technique is particularly effective against simple volumetric attacks.

- Geo-blocking: Given that DDoS attacks often originate from specific regions, cloud services can block or limit traffic from geographic locations known for harboring attackers.

- Web Application Firewalls (WAFs): Deployed within cloud services, WAFs scrutinize HTTP/HTTPS traffic for malicious requests and can block attack vectors targeting application layer vulnerabilities.

- Anycast Network Diffusion: Cloud services often employ Anycast routing, wherein a single IP address is shared across multiple servers around the globe. This not only accelerates content delivery to legitimate users but also disperses and dilutes DDoS attack traffic across a broader network, significantly reducing its impact.

- Behavioural Analysis: By constantly analyzing the behavior of incoming traffic, cloud services can identify and mitigate sophisticated attacks designed to mimic legitimate user behavior, such as Slowloris or HTTP flood attacks.

One of the cloud's most formidable attributes in the context of DDoS defense is its capacity for continuous adaptation. Cloud providers invest heavily in research and development to stay abreast of emerging DDoS tactics and techniques. This commitment ensures that their mitigation strategies evolve in tandem with the threats, offering a dynamic defense mechanism that can adapt to counter new and unforeseen attack vectors.

Beyond individual cloud platforms, the broader ecosystem

of cloud services contributes to a collective defense against DDoS threats. Through shared threat intelligence networks, cloud providers exchange data on emerging DDoS patterns and attacker tactics, enriching their defensive strategies. This collaborative approach amplifies the resilience of the cloud, making it an ever-more formidable adversary against the scourge of DDoS attacks.

the role of cloud services in absorbing and mitigating DDoS attacks is multifaceted and indispensable. Through a blend of massive absorption capacity, advanced traffic analysis, strategic mitigation techniques, continuous adaptation, and collaborative defense, cloud services offer a bulwark against the disruption and damage wrought by DDoS attacks. As cyber threats continue to evolve, the cloud's role in cyber defense will only grow in importance, underscoring the need for organizations to integrate cloud-based DDoS protection into their broader cybersecurity strategy.

Evaluating and Choosing the Right Cloud Provider for DDoS Protection

Before embarking on the quest for the right cloud provider, it's imperative to conduct an introspective examination of your organization's specific needs and vulnerabilities. Understanding the scale of your operations, the nature of your digital assets, and the potential impact of DDoS attacks on your business are foundational steps. This self-assessment guides the prioritization of features and services in a cloud provider, be it expansive bandwidth, advanced traffic filtering, or geographic reach.

The cornerstone of a cloud provider's defense against DDoS attacks lies in its mitigation capabilities. When evaluating providers, delve into the specifics of their DDoS mitigation technology, including the scale of attacks they can absorb, the diversity of attacks they can counteract (volumetric, protocol, application layer), and the speed at which they can mitigate an attack. The provider's historical performance during real-world DDoS attacks provides invaluable insights into their effectiveness and reliability.

In the dynamic digital arena, the ability of a cloud provider to scale resources on demand is vital. The provider must offer scalable DDoS protection that aligns with the growth of your business and the evolution of cyber threats. Flexibility in adjusting protection parameters and customizing the response to DDoS attacks based on your changing needs is a significant consideration.

While DDoS protection is paramount, it should not come at the expense of network performance. Evaluate the potential latency introduced by the provider's DDoS mitigation mechanisms and their impact on user experience. Providers who manage to balance robust DDoS protection with minimal performance degradation offer a competitive advantage.

Seek out cloud providers who offer transparency in their DDoS mitigation processes and control over the response mechanisms. The ability to access real-time analytics on traffic and threats, along with customizable alerting systems, empowers organizations to maintain situational awareness and adjust defenses as necessary.

The compatibility of the cloud provider's services with your existing infrastructure is crucial for a seamless defense strategy. Consider providers who offer easy integration options and support for a hybrid cloud environment, ensuring that DDoS protection extends cohesively across all aspects of your digital footprint.

The quality of support provided by a cloud service is indicative of their partnership in your defense strategy. Providers who offer 24/7 support, dedicated account management, and proactive threat intelligence sharing demonstrate a commitment to not just selling a service, but to fortifying your organization's defenses.

Finally, while cost should not be the primary factor in selecting a cloud provider for DDoS protection, it is an unavoidable consideration. Analyze the provider's pricing structure, looking for transparency and alignment with your expected usage and protection needs. Beware of hidden costs associated with scaling protection services or responding to an actual DDoS attack.

choosing the right cloud provider for DDoS protection is a multifaceted decision that extends beyond mere technical capabilities. It requires a holistic assessment of the provider's alignment with your organization's specific needs, operational ethos, and long-term cybersecurity strategy. Through meticulous evaluation and strategic selection, organizations can forge a partnership with a cloud provider that not only shields them from the ravages of DDoS attacks but also supports their growth and digital transformation journey in the safe harbor of robust cybersecurity defenses.

CHAPTER 6:
ENGAGING EXTERNAL
SUPPORT AND
SERVICES

I SPs, are often the first to detect unusual patterns that may signify an impending DDoS attack. Through the implementation of sophisticated monitoring systems, ISPs can alert businesses to these anomalies, facilitating an early response that can prevent or mitigate the attack's impact.

One of the most effective strategies against a DDoS attack is the diversion of traffic away from the targeted site. ISPs are adept at rerouting this deluge through various mechanisms, such as scrubbing centers where bad traffic is "cleaned" before being sent to its intended destination. This technique ensures that only legitimate traffic reaches the business, thereby maintaining its online presence and operations.

Rate limiting is another potent tool in the ISP arsenal. By controlling the rate at which requests are made to a server, ISPs can prevent the server from becoming overwhelmed by excessive demands, a common tactic in DDoS attacks. This approach not only safeguards the targeted website but also ensures the equitable distribution of network resources among all users.

Beyond these technical strategies, the relationship between businesses and ISPs is also defined by a mutual commitment to security. ISPs can offer guidance on best practices for DDoS prevention, tailored to the specific vulnerabilities and needs of the business. Furthermore, this partnership fosters a continuous exchange of information, allowing both parties to stay ahead of emerging threats.

Integral to this collaboration are Service Level Agreements (SLAs) between businesses and ISPs. These agreements outline the expectations and responsibilities of each party in the event of a DDoS attack, including response times, mitigation strategies, and communication protocols. SLAs ensure a clear, contractual commitment to defense against DDoS attacks, providing businesses with peace of mind and a measure of accountability from their ISP.

In the digital arena, where DDoS attacks loom as a persistent threat, the alliance between businesses and Internet Service Providers is indispensable. Through early detection, traffic management, and shared commitment to security, ISPs play a pivotal role in fortifying the cyber defenses of businesses. This partnership not only enhances the resilience of individual companies but also contributes to the broader effort to maintain the integrity and reliability of the internet as a whole.

As we navigate the complexities of cybersecurity, the collaboration between businesses and ISPs exemplifies a united front against DDoS attacks, embodying the principles of vigilance, innovation, and collective action that are essential in securing our digital future.

How ISPs Can Help Mitigate DDoS Attacks

Leveraging advanced algorithms and machine learning technologies, ISPs can conduct sophisticated traffic analysis to distinguish between legitimate user activity and potential DDoS attack patterns. This early detection system is paramount, as it enables ISPs to identify and address threats before they escalate into full-blown attacks. Through continuous monitoring of data packets and analyzing their sources, sizes, and frequencies, ISPs can pinpoint anomalies that deviate from normal traffic behavior, facilitating swift intervention.

In response to identified threats, ISPs can implement geo-blocking or IP blacklisting strategies to block traffic originating from suspicious or malicious sources. Geo-blocking restricts access to the targeted resource from specific geographical locations known to harbor cyber attackers, while IP blacklisting denies access to individual IP addresses or ranges involved in the attack. These measures, although sometimes controversial due to their broad impact, serve as powerful tools in neutralizing the sources of DDoS traffic.

The robust infrastructure of ISPs allows for scalability and elasticity in handling internet traffic. During a DDoS attack, the demand on the target's bandwidth can skyrocket exponentially. ISPs, with their extensive network resources, can absorb or dilute the impact of increased traffic, preventing the targeted servers from becoming overwhelmed. This capacity for traffic accommodation is critical in maintaining the availability of online services amidst a DDoS onslaught.

ISPs are pivotal in fostering collaborative defense strategies against DDoS attacks. By sharing threat intelligence and attack signatures with other ISPs and cybersecurity entities, they contribute to a collective knowledge base that enhances the detection and prevention of DDoS attacks on a global scale. This communal approach not only strengthens individual defenses but also creates a more secure and resilient internet infrastructure.

Many ISPs offer specialized DDoS mitigation services as part of their portfolio, providing businesses with an added layer of protection. These services typically include a combination of the strategies mentioned above, along with bespoke solutions tailored to the specific needs and vulnerabilities of the client. By leveraging the expertise and resources of their ISP for DDoS mitigation, businesses can significantly bolster their defenses against this pervasive threat.

The proactive and reactive measures taken by ISPs are vital in the battle against DDoS attacks. From advanced traffic analysis to the implementation of scalable solutions and collaborative defense strategies, ISPs equip businesses with the tools necessary to withstand and recover from these cyber assaults. As the landscape of cyber threats evolves, the dynamic role of ISPs in mitigating DDoS attacks will continue to expand, underscoring the importance of their partnership with businesses in securing the digital domain. Through these concerted efforts, ISPs not only safeguard individual clients but also contribute to the stability and resilience of the internet as a whole, fortifying our collective defense against the scourge of DDoS attacks.

Negotiating Appropriate Service Level Agreements (SLAs) for DDoS Protection

A Service Level Agreement (SLA) is a contractual commitment between a service provider and a client that specifies the levels of service to be delivered. Within the context of DDoS protection, an SLA becomes a pivotal document that outlines the responsibilities of the ISP in mitigating and responding to DDoS attacks, delineating metrics such as response time, mitigation strategies, and uptime guarantees.

When negotiating an SLA for DDoS protection, certain components are essential to ensure comprehensive coverage and clear expectations. These include:

- Response Time: The SLA should specify the maximum response time from the ISP upon detection of a DDoS attack, ensuring swift action to minimize damage.

- Uptime Guarantees: A critical metric for any online business, this outlines the expected availability of services, expressed as a percentage of total time across a specified period.

- Attack Detection: Details on how the ISP will detect DDoS attacks, including the technologies and methodologies employed, are vital for transparency and preparedness.

- Mitigation Strategies: The SLA should clearly describe the mitigation strategies that the ISP will deploy to combat DDoS attacks, including traffic filtering, rate limiting, and IP blacklisting.

- Reporting and Communication: A provision for regular reports on potential threats, ongoing attacks, and post-attack analysis ensures that the client is well-informed and can act accordingly.

- Compensation and Penalties: Clauses detailing compensation for SLA breaches, such as refunds or credits, provide accountability and assurance for the client.

Negotiating an SLA for DDoS protection is a collaborative process that requires a thorough understanding of one's business needs, risk assessment, and the technical capabilities of the ISP. It involves:

- Assessment of Needs: Identifying the specific DDoS protection requirements based on the organization's digital footprint, critical assets, and potential risk exposure.

- Market Research: Evaluating the DDoS mitigation services offered by various ISPs, focusing on their track record, technological prowess, and customer testimonials.

- Dialogue and Tailoring: Engaging with ISPs to discuss specific needs, asking for customizations in the service offering to better address the unique challenges faced by the business.

- Review and Adjustment: Carefully reviewing the proposed SLA, seeking clarifications, and requesting adjustments to ensure that all critical aspects of DDoS protection are adequately covered.

In the realm of cybersecurity, where the threat landscape is continually evolving, securing a well-crafted SLA for DDoS protection with an ISP is not just a matter of operational necessity but also a strategic asset. It ensures that businesses have a clear framework for response and recovery in the event of a DDoS attack, minimizing potential disruptions and safeguarding their digital integrity. As businesses negotiate these agreements, they fortify their defenses against the cyber threats of tomorrow, ensuring resilience and continuity in the face of adversity. Through diligent negotiation and strategic foresight, organizations can navigate the complexities of cyber risk, transforming potential vulnerabilities into bastions of strength.

Collaborative Efforts Between Businesses and ISPs in DDoS Defense

At the heart of effective DDoS defense lies a synergistic approach where businesses and ISPs operate not as separate entities but as allies against a common adversary. This partnership leverages the unique strengths of each party to create a multi-layered defense strategy, enhancing the overall resilience of the digital infrastructure.

Businesses are tasked with implementing robust internal cybersecurity policies, including but not limited to, secure network architecture, regular security audits, and employee training programs. These measures are designed to reduce vulnerabilities and mitigate the impact of attacks.

ISPs, on the other hand, bring to the table sophisticated detection and mitigation tools that can identify and respond to DDoS threats at the network level. Their role extends to providing high-capacity bandwidth to absorb volumetric attacks, employing advanced filtering techniques to weed out malicious traffic, and offering on-demand scalability to handle unexpected surges.

1. Communication and Information Sharing: Establishing open lines of communication for the swift exchange of threat intelligence and real-time information during an attack. This

includes setting up dedicated points of contact and secure communication channels.

2. Joint Risk Assessment: Conducting collaborative assessments to identify potential vulnerabilities, evaluate the risk landscape, and prioritize defense mechanisms based on the criticality of assets and the likelihood of threats.

3. Customized Mitigation Plans: Working together to develop tailored DDoS mitigation strategies that align with the business's specific needs, operational dynamics, and risk tolerance levels. This involves mapping out response protocols, escalation procedures, and recovery plans.

4. Regular Drills and Simulations: Conducting joint exercises to simulate DDoS attack scenarios, testing the effectiveness of response strategies, and ensuring that both parties are prepared to act swiftly and cohesively in the event of an actual attack.

5. Innovative Collaboration: Exploring new technologies and methodologies, such as blockchain for decentralized threat intelligence sharing or AI-driven anomaly detection systems, to stay ahead of evolving DDoS tactics.

Highlighting real-world examples where collaborative efforts between businesses and ISPs have successfully thwarted DDoS attacks can provide valuable insights and best practices. These case studies underscore the importance of a proactive and cooperative stance in cybersecurity, showcasing how leveraging collective resources and expertise can lead to stronger defenses and minimized disruptions.

Despite the clear benefits, collaborative defense efforts are not without challenges. These range from logistical issues, such as aligning different operational procedures and protocols, to legal and privacy concerns related to data sharing. Overcoming these obstacles requires a commitment to transparency, mutual respect, and a shared vision for a more secure cyber environment.

The battle against DDoS attacks is continuous and ever-evolving, making the collaborative efforts between businesses and ISPs not just beneficial but essential. By forging strong partnerships and leveraging each other's strengths, they can create a formidable barrier against cyber threats. This cooperative model not only enhances the individual security posture of each entity but also contributes to the broader goal of creating a safer, more resilient digital ecosystem. Through mutual support and shared initiatives, businesses and ISPs can turn the tide against DDoS attackers, protecting critical digital assets and ensuring the uninterrupted flow of the digital economy.

The Role of DDoS Mitigation Services

DDoS mitigation services specialize in protecting networks, servers, and applications from distributed denial-of-service (DDoS) attacks. By employing a sophisticated array of countermeasures, these services detect, analyze, and mitigate malicious traffic before it reaches the intended target, thereby ensuring uninterrupted business operations.

1. Detection: The first line of defense involves accurately identifying an incoming DDoS attack from regular spikes in traffic. This is achieved through continuous monitoring of traffic flows and leveraging advanced algorithms to discern patterns indicative of an attack.

2. Response: Upon detection, DDoS mitigation services swiftly

react to neutralize the threat. This rapid response is facilitated by pre-configured defensive measures tailored to the specific attributes and severity of the attack.

3. Diversion: One common tactic is traffic diversion, where incoming traffic is rerouted through the mitigation service's scrubbing centers. These centers cleanse the traffic by filtering out malicious packets, allowing only legitimate traffic to pass through.

4. Analysis and Adaptation: Post-attack, the service conducts a thorough analysis to understand the attack vectors and techniques used. Insights garnered from this analysis feed into the continuous improvement of defense mechanisms, ensuring preparedness for future attacks.

- Volumetric Attack Mitigation: Combats large-scale attempts to saturate bandwidth, utilizing techniques such as rate limiting and traffic shaping.

- Protocol Attack Mitigation: Addresses attacks targeting network infrastructure, through packet inspection and filtering.

- Application Layer Attack Mitigation: Protects against sophisticated attacks aimed at web applications by analyzing and scrubbing HTTP traffic.

Choosing the right DDoS mitigation service is critical. Factors to consider include:

- Capacity: The service's ability to handle large-scale attacks without faltering.

- Responsiveness: The speed at which the service can detect and respond to an attack.

- Flexibility: The service's adaptability to evolving attack vectors and techniques.

- Integration: How seamlessly the service integrates with existing security infrastructure.

Illustrative case studies of businesses that have successfully thwarted DDoS attacks with the help of mitigation services underscore the value these services provide. These narratives not only highlight the efficacy of specific mitigation strategies but also demonstrate the importance of proactive engagement with DDoS mitigation services.

The role of DDoS mitigation services in today's cybersecurity landscape cannot be overstated. As the frequency and complexity of DDoS attacks continue to escalate, these services stand on the front lines, defending the digital domain against disruption. Their expertise in swiftly identifying, mitigating, and analyzing DDoS threats is invaluable for businesses striving to maintain operational continuity in the face of cyber adversity. By partnering with a reputable DDoS mitigation service, businesses can fortify their defenses, ensuring resilience against the ever-present threat of denial-of-service attacks.

Overview of Third-Party DDoS Mitigation Services

Third-party DDoS mitigation services are specialized entities that offer DDoS protection as an outsourced service. Unlike in-house solutions that require substantial resources and expertise to manage, third-party services offer a cost-effective, scalable, and expert-driven alternative. By positioning themselves as intermediaries between an organization's network and the wider internet, they can effectively shield their clients from the brunt of DDoS attacks.

These services employ a multi-faceted approach to DDoS mitigation, incorporating various strategies such as:

- Anycast Network Distribution: Utilizing a global network of distributed servers, these services disperse incoming traffic across multiple points of presence (PoPs), diluting the impact of an attack.

- Advanced Traffic Scrubbing: Sophisticated algorithms and filtering technologies are deployed to distinguish between legitimate traffic and malicious data packets, ensuring that only clean traffic reaches the client's infrastructure.

- Behavioral Analysis: Leveraging machine learning and AI, third-party services continuously analyze traffic patterns to detect anomalies that may signify emerging threats, allowing for preemptive action.

- Expertise and Focus: Specialization in DDoS mitigation means that these services are equipped with the latest knowledge and technologies to combat attacks.

- Cost Efficiency: Outsourcing to a third-party provider can be more economical than developing and maintaining an in-house capability.

- Scalability: As businesses grow, third-party services can easily scale their protection mechanisms to accommodate increased traffic and evolving security needs.

- 24/7 Monitoring and Support: Continuous monitoring ensures that threats are identified and mitigated swiftly, minimizing potential downtime.

When selecting a third-party DDoS mitigation service, organizations should evaluate:

- Service Level Agreements (SLAs): Clear SLAs are crucial for defining the expectations and responsibilities of the third-party service, including attack detection times, mitigation commencement, and overall uptime guarantees.

- Customization and Control: The ability to tailor the service to specific needs and maintain a degree of control over the mitigation process.

- Transparency and Reporting: Insight into attack analytics and mitigation actions, fostering a transparent relationship between the service provider and the client.

- Compatibility: The service's compatibility with the organization's existing security infrastructure and its ability to integrate seamlessly.

The landscape of third-party DDoS mitigation services is vast, with each offering varying levels of protection, customization, and support. Organizations must conduct a thorough assessment of their specific needs, vulnerabilities, and budgetary constraints to identify a service that not only aligns with their operational requirements but also enhances their cybersecurity posture.

In the face of increasingly sophisticated DDoS attacks, the role of third-party mitigation services is more critical than ever. As these threats evolve, so too must the strategies and technologies deployed to counter them. By partnering with a third-party DDoS mitigation service, organizations can leverage expert knowledge and advanced technologies to safeguard their digital assets, ensuring resilience in an unpredictable cyber landscape. Through this collaborative approach, the future of cybersecurity becomes a shared endeavor, fortified by the collective expertise and innovative solutions offered by third-party mitigation services.

Criteria for Selecting a DDoS Mitigation Service

The cornerstone of an effective DDoS mitigation service is its ability to offer comprehensive protection across various attack vectors. Organizations should seek services that provide:

- Broad-Spectrum Coverage: Capability to mitigate a wide range of DDoS attacks, including volumetric, protocol, and application layer attacks.

- High-Capacity Bandwidth: Adequate bandwidth to absorb large-scale DDoS attacks without compromising the normal function of the network.

- Adaptive Threat Intelligence: Utilization of real-time threat intelligence to adapt protections against evolving DDoS tactics.

The efficacy of a DDoS mitigation service is measured by its performance and reliability under fire. Key performance indicators include:

- Low Latency: Ensuring that the addition of DDoS protection does not introduce significant latency to normal traffic flow.

- High Availability: Infrastructure that guarantees service availability, even during complex, multi-vector DDoS attacks.

- Rapid Response Time: The speed at which the service can detect and start mitigating an attack is crucial. Services offering near-instantaneous response times are preferable.

As organizations grow, so too do their digital footprints and security needs. The right DDoS mitigation service must, therefore, offer:

- Scalable Solutions: The ability to scale protection measures up or down based on the intensity of the attack and the growth of the business.

- Flexible Deployment Options: Options for on-premise, cloud-based, or hybrid deployment models to fit the organization's infrastructure and security requirements.

Visibility into attack details and mitigation actions is vital for organizations to understand and evolve their defense strategies. A suitable DDoS mitigation service should provide:

- Real-Time Alerts and Notifications: Immediate notification of potential and ongoing attacks, allowing for swift decision-making.

- Detailed Reporting: Post-attack reports containing comprehensive details about the attack vectors used, the duration of the attack, and the mitigation techniques that were employed.

- Actionable Insights: Analysis and recommendations for improving security posture based on attack patterns and vulnerabilities exploited.

While cybersecurity is paramount, organizations must also consider their budgetary constraints. Evaluating the cost-effectiveness of a DDoS mitigation service involves:

- Transparent Pricing Models: Clear and predictable pricing structures without hidden fees.

- Value for Money: Assessment of the service's features, performance, and reliability against its cost.

- Customizable Plans: Availability of customizable plans that allow organizations to pay only for the services they need.

The credibility of a DDoS mitigation service provider is crucial. Organizations should consider:

- Industry Experience: Providers with a proven track record and expertise in DDoS mitigation.

- Customer Support: Access to 24/7 customer support with technical experts who can assist during and after an attack.

- Client Testimonials and Case Studies: Insight from other organizations' experiences can provide valuable information on the provider's capabilities and reliability.

Selecting a DDoS mitigation service is a decision that should not be taken lightly. By carefully considering these criteria, organizations can partner with a service that not only protects their digital assets but also aligns with their operational needs and budgetary constraints. In the dynamic battlefield of cybersecurity, having a trusted, capable, and responsive DDoS mitigation partner is indispensable for maintaining resilience in the face of relentless cyber threats.

Real-World Examples of Effective Mitigation During an Attack

In a meticulously orchestrated assault, a leading financial institution became the target of a sophisticated DDoS attack aimed at crippling its online banking services. The attackers deployed a multi-vector strategy, simultaneously unleashing volumetric attacks that flooded the network and application layer attacks that sought to exhaust server resources.

Mitigation Strategy: The institution's rapid response team, equipped with advanced DDoS protection tools, immediately identified the anomalous traffic patterns. Utilizing a cloud-based DDoS mitigation service, they were able to re-route the malicious traffic away from their network, effectively nullifying the attack's impact. The implementation of rate-limiting and IP reputation filtering further helped in distinguishing and blocking nefarious traffic, ensuring uninterrupted service to legitimate users.

Outcome: The financial institution's preemptive cybersecurity measures and the swift activation of its DDoS mitigation protocols ensured that the attack was neutralized with minimal service disruption. This incident highlights the efficacy of cloud-based mitigation services and the criticality of real-time traffic analysis.

During a peak shopping season, an online retailer experienced a sudden and dramatic surge in traffic, a hallmark of a well-timed DDoS attack designed to disrupt operations and erode consumer trust. The attack's complexity was evident in its execution, employing a blend of high-volume traffic to overwhelm bandwidth and meticulously crafted requests to target application-layer vulnerabilities.

Mitigation Strategy: Leveraging an on-premise DDoS mitigation appliance in conjunction with a secondary, cloud-based mitigation service provided a robust, layered defense. The on-premise appliance scrutinized incoming traffic for anomalies, while the cloud service acted as an overflow valve, absorbing and analyzing excessive traffic volumes. This hybrid approach enabled the retailer to maintain its online presence, mitigating the attack without sacrificing customer experience.

Outcome: Through the deployment of a hybrid DDoS mitigation strategy, the retailer successfully thwarted the attack, safeguarding its sales and reputation during a critical business period. This case illustrates the flexibility and effectiveness of combining on-premise and cloud-based solutions to defend against sophisticated cyber threats.

A popular online gaming platform became the target of a relentless DDoS campaign, experiencing multiple waves of attacks aimed at saturating its servers and disrupting its service. The attackers exploited a variety of techniques, from amplification attacks exploiting vulnerable UDP protocols to sophisticated application-layer attacks.

Mitigation Strategy: The gaming company employed a multifaceted defense strategy, incorporating anomaly detection systems to quickly identify and mitigate unusual traffic patterns. A global content delivery network (CDN) played a pivotal role in absorbing and dispersing attack traffic, leveraging its distributed nature to minimize latency and maintain service availability. Simultaneously, the use of Web Application Firewalls (WAFs) protected against application-layer attacks by filtering and blocking malicious requests.

Outcome: The comprehensive defensive measures adopted by the gaming platform were instrumental in mitigating the DDoS attacks. The ability to absorb and disperse attack traffic through a CDN, combined with the targeted protection offered by WAFs, ensured uninterrupted service and a secure gaming experience for users.

These real-world examples underscore the complexity and variability of DDoS attacks and the necessity for adaptive, multi-layered mitigation strategies. From financial institutions to online retailers and gaming platforms, the keys to successful defense include preparedness, a robust infrastructure capable of absorbing and analyzing attack traffic, and the strategic deployment of on-premise and cloud-based mitigation solutions. As cyber threats continue to evolve, so too must our approaches to cybersecurity, ensuring that resilience becomes a hallmark of our digital age.

Legal and Regulatory Considerations in the Context of DDoS Attacks

The legality of cyber actions, including DDoS attacks, varies significantly across jurisdictions, but there's a growing consensus on viewing such attacks as criminal acts. For instance, in the United States, the Computer Fraud and Abuse

Act (CFAA) serves as the primary federal statute to prosecute cybercrimes, under which DDoS attacks can be classified as unauthorized access to a computer network. Similarly, in the European Union, the Directive on Attacks against Information Systems explicitly criminalizes the intentional disruption of information systems, covering DDoS attacks.

Key Legal Considerations:

- Jurisdictional Challenges: The cross-border nature of DDoS attacks poses significant jurisdictional challenges, complicating the legal response. Attackers can launch assaults from any global location, complicating the process of legal recourse and prosecution.

- Proving Intent: A crucial legal hurdle in prosecuting DDoS attacks is proving the intent behind the attack, a requirement for establishing criminal liability.

- Collateral Damage: Legal considerations also extend to potential collateral damage caused by a DDoS attack, including data breaches or loss, and the subsequent liabilities organizations might face towards third parties.

Beyond the legal implications, organizations must also adhere to a plethora of regulatory requirements that mandate specific cybersecurity measures, including protection against DDoS attacks. Non-compliance with these regulations can result in hefty fines and reputational damage.

Critical Regulatory Frameworks:

- General Data Protection Regulation (GDPR): For organizations operating within or handling data from the European Union, GDPR mandates stringent data protection measures. While not specifically mentioning DDoS, the regulation requires the implementation of appropriate technical measures to ensure data security, which implicitly includes DDoS mitigation strategies.

- Health Insurance Portability and Accountability Act (HIPAA): In the healthcare sector, HIPAA requires the protection of patient data against cyber threats, necessitating healthcare providers to implement DDoS mitigation techniques as part of their cybersecurity measures.

- Financial Industry Regulatory Authority (FINRA): Financial institutions are under the scrutiny of various regulatory bodies, including FINRA, which mandates comprehensive cybersecurity practices to protect against threats like DDoS attacks.

Organizations must develop a proactive approach to navigate the legal and regulatory landscape effectively:

- Legal Expertise: Engaging with legal experts specializing in cyber law can provide valuable insights into the legal obligations and strategies for compliance and defense.

- Regulatory Compliance Programs: Establishing comprehensive compliance programs that address the spectrum of regulatory requirements relevant to the organization's operation is crucial.

- Incident Response Planning: Effective incident response plans should include not just technical response mechanisms but also legal and communication strategies to address potential legal ramifications post-attack.

The fight against DDoS attacks is waged on multiple fronts, including the legal and regulatory arenas. Understanding and complying with the evolving legal landscape and regulatory requirements are as crucial as implementing technological defenses. Organizations must adopt a holistic approach, integrating legal compliance and cybersecurity practices to navigate the complexities of DDoS mitigation successfully. As the digital realm continues to evolve, so too will the legal and regulatory frameworks governing it, requiring ongoing vigilance and adaptation from all entities operating within this space.

Understanding the Legal Landscape Regarding DDoS Attacks

At the heart of the legal response to DDoS attacks is the task of definition and classification. While the specific legal nomenclature may vary, the consensus categorizes DDoS attacks under unauthorized access, use, or disruption of computer systems. For instance, in the United States, such actions are prosecutable under the Computer Fraud and Abuse Act (CFAA), which penalizes those who intentionally access a computer without authorization or exceed authorized access.

In contrast, the European Union's Directive on Attacks against Information Systems offers a broader scope, explicitly criminalizing the intentional disruption of information systems through attacks like DDoS. These legal definitions form the foundation upon which prosecutions and defense strategies are built, highlighting the importance of precise legal interpretation in the realm of cyber law.

One of the most daunting aspects of tackling DDoS attacks from a legal standpoint is their inherently international nature. Attackers can, and often do, launch their assaults from jurisdictions beyond the reach of victims' national laws, creating a web of international legal challenges. This cross-border aspect necessitates international cooperation and treaties, such as the Budapest Convention on Cybercrime, which aims to harmonize legal frameworks and foster international collaboration in combating cybercrime, including DDoS attacks.

Legal precedents play a critical role in shaping the judicial approach to DDoS attacks. Notable cases, such as the prosecution of the individuals behind the Operation Payback DDoS attacks, serve as benchmarks for legal action against similar future incidents. These precedents not only guide legal professionals in building cases but also help organizations understand the potential legal consequences of failing to secure their networks against DDoS threats.

Beyond the direct legal implications of falling victim to or unintentionally facilitating a DDoS attack, organizations must also navigate a labyrinth of compliance obligations. Regulations such as the General Data Protection Regulation (GDPR) in the European Union and the Health Insurance Portability and Accountability Act (HIPAA) in the United States impose strict requirements on data protection and cybersecurity measures. While not explicitly focusing on DDoS, these regulations mandate the implementation of comprehensive security measures, indirectly covering defenses against such attacks.

For organizations, the path through the legal landscape of DDoS attacks involves several key strategies:

- Legal Consultation: Regular consultation with cyber law experts can provide organizations with up-to-date information on legal and regulatory changes, ensuring readiness to respond to or prevent DDoS attacks within the legal framework.

- Proactive Compliance: Staying ahead of regulatory requirements by implementing robust cybersecurity measures can mitigate the risk of non-compliance penalties and provide a stronger defense in the event of legal action following a DDoS attack.

- International Cooperation: Engaging in and supporting international efforts to combat cybercrime can enhance an organization's ability to respond to and recover from DDoS attacks, leveraging global resources and intelligence.

The legal landscape surrounding DDoS attacks is a complex and ever-evolving field, requiring a nuanced understanding of both national and international law. As organizations strive to protect themselves against these cyber threats, integrating legal considerations into their cybersecurity strategies is essential. By navigating the legal and regulatory frameworks with informed precision, entities can bolster their defenses and ensure a more secure and compliant operational posture in the digital age.

Reporting Requirements and Cooperation with Law Enforcement

The obligation to report a DDoS attack is not universally standardized and varies significantly across jurisdictions. In some countries, laws or regulations mandate the reporting of cyber incidents to national cyber authorities or law enforcement agencies. For example, in the United States, the Cybersecurity and Infrastructure Security Agency (CISA) recommends reporting incidents to help understand cyber threats and provide assistance. Similarly, the European Union's NIS Directive obligates operators of essential services and digital service providers to notify national authorities about significant cyber incidents.

The variance in reporting requirements underscores the necessity for organizations to familiarize themselves with the laws applicable in their jurisdictions and sectors. Failure to comply with these reporting obligations can lead to legal repercussions, including fines and penalties, underscoring the importance of adherence.

The effectiveness of law enforcement's response to DDoS attacks is heavily reliant on the timely and accurate reporting from the victims. Swift reporting can aid in the mitigation of the attack, preservation of vital evidence, and potentially, the identification and prosecution of the perpetrators. It provides authorities with critical insights into attack vectors, trends, and techniques, contributing to a broader defense strategy against future attacks.

Organizations should establish protocols for incident reporting, detailing when, how, and to whom cyber incidents should be reported. Such protocols ensure that during the tumultuous period following an attack, steps are taken efficiently and effectively, maximizing the potential for a positive outcome.

Engagement with law enforcement goes beyond mere reporting; it encompasses a full spectrum of cooperation. This partnership can range from sharing detailed incident data to aiding in investigations through the provision of access to systems or logs. Law enforcement agencies, in turn, can offer technical assistance, advice on mitigating damage, and, crucially, information on broader threat landscapes that might affect the organization in the future.

For many organizations, cooperation with law enforcement is a nuanced decision, balancing the benefits of external assistance and the protection of privacy and sensitive information. Clear communication and understanding of mutual goals and boundaries are essential in this cooperation, facilitated by legal counsel when necessary.

The foundation of effective reporting and cooperation with law enforcement is built on prior engagement and relationship building. Organizations are encouraged to establish contact with relevant cybercrime units before incidents occur. Participating in cybersecurity forums, initiatives, and working groups can also enhance mutual understanding and foster a community approach to combating cyber threats.

The landscape of DDoS attacks is fraught with challenges, not least of which is navigating the aftermath in a legal and cooperative context. Understanding the obligations for reporting and the value of cooperation with law enforcement agencies is crucial for any organization. By fostering a proactive approach to these responsibilities, entities can contribute to a more robust and resilient cybersecurity ecosystem, benefiting not only themselves but the wider community in the face of ever-evolving cyber threats.

International Collaboration and Its Importance in Combating DDOS Attacks

The fabric of international collaboration in combating DDoS attacks is composed of several threads, each integral to the overarching tapestry of global cybersecurity. At the forefront is the exchange of threat intelligence. Cybercriminals operate with a degree of anonymity and fluidity that is unbounded by geographic constraints, leveraging resources and vulnerabilities across the globe. In response, nations and organizations must reciprocate by fostering an environment of open communication and sharing of intelligence. This symbiotic exchange encompasses real-time alerts on emerging threats, technical insights on attack methodologies, and strategic advice on mitigation techniques. By pooling resources and knowledge, the global community can anticipate and counteract DDoS campaigns with greater agility and precision.

Moreover, the establishment of international cybersecurity frameworks plays a pivotal role. These agreements, often forged under the auspices of multinational entities such as the United Nations or the International Telecommunication Union, aim to harmonize cyber defense strategies, establish common standards, and promote best practices. Through these frameworks, countries can align their legal and regulatory landscapes, thereby closing the loopholes that cybercriminals exploit. Additionally, these alliances facilitate coordinated responses to large-scale DDoS attacks, enabling a synchronized deployment of defensive measures that amplifies their efficacy.

Training and capacity building represent another critical facet of international cooperation. Developing nations, in particular, may lack the resources or expertise to effectively combat sophisticated DDoS attacks. Through collaborative programs, more technologically advanced countries can provide training, technical support, and resources to bolster the cyber resilience of their global counterparts. This not only uplifts the cybersecurity posture of individual nations but also strengthens the collective defense against common adversaries.

However, the path to seamless international collaboration is fraught with challenges. Sovereignty concerns, geopolitical tensions, and disparities in cybersecurity maturity levels can impede the flow of information and resources. Overcoming these barriers requires building trust, fostering mutual respect, and recognizing the interdependent nature of cybersecurity in a hyperconnected world.

The battle against DDoS attacks is not confined within national borders; it is a global crusade that demands a concerted effort. International collaboration emerges as a linchpin in this endeavor, offering a beacon of hope in navigating the turbulent waters of cyber warfare. By embracing the principles of cooperation, information sharing, and capacity building, the global community can erect a formidable bulwark against the scourge of DDoS attacks, safeguarding our digital future.

CHAPTER 7: ANALYZING THE ATTACK

T
he initial phase involves gathering logs from various sources including network devices, firewalls, intrusion detection systems (IDS), and servers. This data mosaic provides a timeline of events, revealing the attack's onset, duration, intensity, and cessation. Advanced analytical tools and software are employed to sift through this vast dataset, identifying anomalies that signify malicious activity. Such tools leverage algorithms capable of pattern recognition, flagging irregular traffic flows and pinpointing the origins of the attack.

Deep packet inspection (DPI) plays a crucial role in this investigative journey. DPI allows for the examination of packet payloads, not just header information, providing insights into the specific type of DDoS attack, whether it be volumetric, protocol, or application layer based. This granularity of information is instrumental in understanding the attacker's modus operandi, aiding in the development of targeted mitigation strategies.

Collaboration with internet service providers (ISPs) and

other entities can augment the analysis process. ISPs can offer additional data on traffic patterns and potentially identify the source of spoofed IP addresses. Furthermore, information sharing platforms and cybersecurity forums present opportunities to compare notes with other victims or experts who might have encountered similar attacks, fostering a community-driven approach to problem-solving.

The culmination of this analysis is the formulation of lessons learned. Each attack presents a unique learning opportunity, a chance to adapt and evolve. Security teams meticulously document the findings, translating them into actionable insights. This could involve adjusting thresholds for anomaly-based detection systems, reconfiguring network architecture to enhance resilience, or implementing more robust data filtering mechanisms.

Moreover, post-attack audits are essential to evaluate the effectiveness of the response. This involves scrutinizing the speed and efficacy of the mitigation efforts, the communication flow among stakeholders, and the overall impact on services. Identifying any shortcomings or delays in the response can drive improvements in the cybersecurity incident response plan (IRP).

In navigating the complex landscape of DDoS attack analysis, it is imperative to wield a blend of technical acumen, strategic foresight, and collaborative spirit. By dissecting each attack with meticulous attention to detail, organizations can distill valuable insights, turning adversities into stepping stones towards a more secure digital domain.

Tools and Techniques for Attack Analysis

Network Traffic Analysis Tools: At the forefront of attack analysis are network traffic analysis tools. These powerful solutions monitor incoming and outgoing traffic, identifying patterns indicative of a DDoS attack. Tools such as Wireshark provide deep packet inspection, allowing analysts to delve into the minutiae of each packet, discerning malicious payloads from legitimate traffic. Through real-time analysis and historical data examination, these tools offer invaluable insights into attack vectors, helping to pinpoint the source and nature of the threat.

SIEM Solutions: Security Information and Event Management (SIEM) systems serve as the central nervous system for cybersecurity operations. By aggregating and correlating data from various sources across the network, SIEM solutions offer a holistic view of an organization's security posture. In the context of DDoS attack analysis, SIEM platforms can quickly identify anomalies, automate alerts, and facilitate rapid response. Their ability to integrate with other security tools enhances their utility, making them indispensable for comprehensive attack analysis.

Anomaly Detection Systems: Specialized in identifying deviations from normal behavior, anomaly detection systems are crucial for early detection of DDoS attacks. These systems employ machine learning algorithms to establish a baseline of regular network activity. When an anomaly is detected, such as a sudden surge in traffic to a specific endpoint, the system triggers alerts. This early warning mechanism enables security teams to take preemptive action, potentially thwarting the attack before it can cause significant damage.

Digital Forensics Tools: Post-attack analysis often requires a forensic approach to understand the "how" and "why" behind an attack. Digital forensics tools like X-Ways Forensics and

Autopsy aid in this endeavor, enabling examiners to recover and scrutinize data related to the attack. These tools can unearth remnants of malicious code, trace the steps of the attackers, and provide evidence for legal proceedings if necessary.

Collaborative Intelligence Platforms: No organization is an island in the fight against cyber threats. Collaborative intelligence platforms, such as the Cyber Threat Alliance, foster a shared environment where entities can exchange information on threats, vulnerabilities, and attacks. By leveraging collective intelligence, organizations can benefit from a wider pool of data, gaining insights into attack patterns and mitigation strategies that have proven effective elsewhere.

Stress Testing Services: Understanding the resilience of a network against DDoS attacks is essential. Stress testing services simulate controlled DDoS attacks on an organization's infrastructure, allowing for the assessment of its defenses. This proactive approach identifies vulnerabilities, enabling organizations to fortify their networks against potential attacks.

The symbiosis of these tools and techniques forms the backbone of effective DDoS attack analysis. Through their application, cybersecurity professionals are not only able to dissect and understand past attacks but also fortify their defenses, making their digital domains formidable against future onslaughts. The journey from vulnerability to resilience is paved with knowledge, innovation, and collaborative effort, ensuring that with each attack analyzed, the cybersecurity community grows stronger and more adept at safeguarding the digital landscape.

Lessons Learned and Adapting Strategies Accordingly

Post-Attack Review Meetings: The first step in learning from a DDoS attack is to conduct a comprehensive post-attack review. This involves gathering key stakeholders and security teams to dissect the event meticulously. Questions such as "What was the nature of the attack?", "How did our defenses fare?", and "What could have been done differently?" guide the discussion. This collaborative analysis fosters a culture of transparency and continuous improvement, ensuring that each team member's perspective contributes to a holistic understanding of the incident.

Identifying Security Gaps: A critical outcome of the review meeting is the identification of security gaps that the attack may have exploited. This could range from insufficient network segmentation, outdated security protocols, to overlooked vulnerabilities in third-party services. Acknowledging these gaps is the first step towards remediation, setting the stage for targeted cybersecurity enhancements.

Enhancing Detection Capabilities: One common lesson from DDoS attacks is the need for improved detection capabilities. Many organizations find that their initial detection of the attack was delayed, allowing the attackers to cause more damage than necessary. Leveraging the insights from the attack analysis, security teams can fine-tune their SIEM rules, adjust anomaly detection thresholds, and implement more robust traffic monitoring solutions to ensure faster and more accurate detection of future threats.

Strengthening Mitigation Processes: Analyzing the effectiveness of the mitigation strategies deployed during the attack is another crucial learning point. Did the response plan activate smoothly? Were communication protocols effective? How quickly were services restored? Answering these questions often leads to the development of more robust mitigation tactics, such as automating certain response actions, enhancing coordination with ISPs for traffic filtering, and establishing clearer protocols for internal and external communication during an incident.

Updating Incident Response Plans: The lessons learned from a DDoS attack invariably lead to updates in the organization's incident response plan. This living document must evolve to incorporate new strategies, contact information, and technological solutions identified as necessary during the post-attack review. Regular drills and simulations based on the updated plan are essential to ensure readiness for future incidents.

Fostering a Proactive Security Culture: Beyond technical improvements, one of the most significant lessons from analyzing DDoS attacks is the importance of fostering a proactive security culture. This entails regular training sessions for staff, promoting cybersecurity awareness across all departments, and encouraging a mindset of vigilance and responsibility towards the organization's digital health.

Sharing Knowledge with the Wider Community: Finally, adapting strategies in the wake of a DDoS attack involves sharing lessons learned with the wider cybersecurity community. Whether through industry forums, collaborative intelligence platforms, or cybersecurity consortiums, sharing insights can help others prepare for similar threats, contributing to a collective defense posture that benefits all participants.

The iterative cycle of learning and adaptation that follows a DDoS attack is foundational to cybersecurity resilience. By transforming the insights gleaned from these digital skirmishes into actionable strategies, organizations not only repair their immediate vulnerabilities but also contribute to the creation of a more secure and robust digital ecosystem.

Importance of Post-Attack Audits

Structured Framework for Post-Attack Analysis: The initiation of a post-attack audit is marked by establishing a structured framework that outlines the scope, objectives, and methodologies of the analysis. This framework ensures a comprehensive examination of the attack, covering not only the technical aspects but also the procedural and human factors that might have contributed to the breach. It serves as a blueprint for the audit process, guiding the teams through a methodical exploration of the incident.

Cross-Functional Audit Teams: The complexity of DDoS attacks necessitates the formation of cross-functional audit teams comprising cybersecurity experts, IT personnel, network engineers, and representatives from legal, HR, and communication departments. This multidisciplinary approach facilitates a holistic analysis of the attack, ensuring that all perspectives are considered and that the lessons learned are applicable across the entire organization.

Technical Analysis and Forensics: A significant portion of the post-attack audit is dedicated to technical analysis and digital forensics. This involves dissecting the attack vectors, examining server logs, network traffic, and firewall configurations, and identifying the vulnerabilities exploited. Advanced forensic tools are employed to trace the origins of the attack, understand the attackers' movements within the network, and uncover any malware or tools they might have left behind.

Review of Incident Response Efficacy: An integral part of the audit is evaluating the efficacy of the incident response. This includes assessing the speed and effectiveness of the detection mechanisms, the coordination among response teams, and the impact of the mitigation strategies. It also scrutinizes the communication flow within the organization and with external entities, such as ISPs and cybersecurity services, during the attack.

Documentation and Knowledge Consolidation: The findings of the post-attack audit are meticulously documented, creating a comprehensive archive of the incident. This documentation serves multiple purposes; it acts as a reference for regulatory compliance, aids in legal proceedings if necessary, and becomes a valuable educational tool for training and awareness programs. It also contributes to the knowledge base that will inform future cybersecurity strategies.

Recommendations for Improvement: The culmination of the post-attack audit is the formulation of targeted recommendations for improving the organization's cybersecurity framework. These recommendations may include technical upgrades, policy revisions, training initiatives, and changes to the incident response plan. They are prioritized based on the risk assessment, ensuring that the most critical vulnerabilities are addressed promptly.

Feedback Loops and Continuous Improvement: The audit process establishes feedback loops that integrate the lessons learned into the organization's cybersecurity policies and practices. This continuous improvement cycle is vital for staying ahead of evolving cyber threats. Regular audits, not just in the aftermath of an attack but as part of routine security assessments, become a key component of the organization's cybersecurity strategy.

The importance of post-attack audits extends beyond mere analysis and documentation. It embodies the organization's commitment to learning from adversities, transforming vulnerabilities into strengths, and continuously advancing its cybersecurity defenses. Through rigorous examination, insightful analysis, and the implementation of strategic improvements, post-attack audits are instrumental in building a resilient and secure digital infrastructure capable of withstanding the challenges of tomorrow's cyber landscape.

Restoring Services After a DDoS Attack

Initial Damage Assessment: The first step in the journey towards service restoration is an exhaustive assessment of the damage inflicted by the DDoS attack. This involves identifying the services that were disrupted, the extent of the damage to infrastructure, and any data loss or integrity issues. This assessment acts as the foundation for all subsequent restoration efforts, determining the prioritization of services to be restored based on their criticality to business operations and user impact.

Securing the Environment: Before any attempt to restore services is made, it is crucial to secure the environment against further attacks. This entails patching identified vulnerabilities, changing credentials and security protocols, and possibly enhancing firewall and intrusion detection systems. The goal is to fortify the network's defenses and close any loopholes that the attackers exploited, thereby preventing a recurrence of the attack during the restoration process.

Restoration Planning: With a clear understanding of the damage and a secured environment, the next step is to develop a detailed restoration plan. This plan outlines the sequence of service restoration, taking into account dependencies between services and the need for minimal disruption. It also specifies the resources required for each phase of the restoration, from technical staff to computing and network resources.

Data Integrity Checks and Backups: Before services are brought back online, it is imperative to conduct thorough data integrity checks to ensure that no corrupted data is reintroduced into the system. This may involve validating backup data before restoration and, in some cases, cleansing data to remove any remnants of the attack. The integrity checks are critical in maintaining the trustworthiness and reliability of the restored services.

Phased Restoration: The restoration of services often follows a phased approach, starting with the most critical services. Each service is systematically brought back online after rigorous testing to ensure full functionality and security. This phased restoration allows for the monitoring of system performance and security posture, ensuring that the reintroduction of services does not inadvertently open new vulnerabilities.

Stakeholder Communication: Effective communication with stakeholders, including employees, customers, and partners, is essential throughout the restoration process. This involves providing timely updates on the progress of the restoration, any potential impact on service availability, and measures taken to secure the services. Transparent communication helps in managing expectations and rebuilding trust post-attack.

Post-Restoration Monitoring and Analysis: Once services are restored, a period of intensive monitoring follows. This monitoring is designed to detect any anomalies that could indicate unresolved issues or the presence of latent threats. Additionally, a comprehensive analysis is conducted to evaluate the restoration process, identify lessons learned, and integrate these insights into future contingency planning.

Review and Update of Response Plans: The final step in the service restoration process is a thorough review and update of the organization's incident response and disaster recovery plans. This review leverages the experience gained and the lessons learned from the attack to enhance the organization's resilience and preparedness for future incidents.

Restoring services after a DDoS attack is a nuanced process that requires careful planning, robust security measures, and clear communication. It is a testament to an organization's resilience, showcasing its ability to recover from adversity, learn from the experience, and emerge stronger, with more robust defenses and a renewed commitment to service excellence.

Steps for Safely Restoring Affected Services

Step 1: Establish a Controlled Environment for Restoration: Before embarking on the restoration journey, it's imperative to create a controlled environment. This environment is isolated from the main network to perform safe testing and validation of the affected services. It acts as a buffer zone, preventing any potential threats from impacting the broader network during the restoration process.

Step 2: Prioritize Services for Restoration: Not all services are created equal; some are critical to the organization's core operations while others may be less essential. The restoration process starts with a prioritization of services based on their business criticality, dependency on other services, and impact on stakeholders. This prioritization ensures that resources are allocated efficiently, focusing first on restoring services that are vital to the organization's functioning.

Step 3: Validate and Restore Backups: With priorities set, the next step is to validate the integrity of backups for the prioritized services. This involves ensuring that the backups are recent, uncorrupted, and free from any traces of the attack. Once validated, these backups can be safely restored to the controlled environment. This step is crucial as it determines the foundation upon which the services will be rebuilt.

Step 4: Incremental Restoration and Testing: Restoring services is not a blunt force action but rather a delicate process that involves restoring services incrementally and testing each layer as it's brought back. This includes restoring the database layers first, followed by application logic, and finally the user interface components. After each increment, comprehensive testing is performed to ensure functionality, security, and performance meet the pre-defined standards.

Step 5: Harden Security Measures: As services are restored, it's crucial to harden the security measures based on the lessons learned from the DDoS attack. This may involve implementing stricter firewall rules, enhancing intrusion detection systems, and applying more robust encryption methods. This step is about transforming vulnerabilities into strengths, fortifying the service against future attacks.

Step 6: Gradual Reintegration into the Main Network: Once services have been restored, tested, and secured in the controlled environment, the next step is their gradual reintegration into the main network. This phased approach allows for the monitoring of the services in the live environment, ensuring they operate as expected without introducing new vulnerabilities.

Step 7: Conduct a Post-Mortem Analysis: After the services have been safely restored and reintegrated, a comprehensive post-mortem analysis is conducted. This analysis reviews the entire incident from the onset of the DDoS attack through to the restoration process, identifying what was successful, what wasn't, and why. The findings from this analysis are then used to further refine the incident response and disaster recovery plans.

Step 8: Update Documentation and Train Staff: The final step involves updating all relevant documentation with the details of the incident, the restoration process, and the lessons learned. Additionally, staff training sessions are conducted to disseminate this knowledge, ensuring that the entire organization is prepared and vigilant for future threats.

Safely restoring services after a DDoS attack requires a detailed and disciplined approach, blending technical acumen with strategic foresight. By following these steps, organizations can not only recover from the immediate aftermath of an attack but also enhance their overall security posture, making them more resilient against future threats.

Communicating with Stakeholders During Recovery

Initial Assessment and Message Development: The first step involves conducting an initial assessment of the attack's impact and developing a clear, concise message that outlines what has happened, the expected impact, and the steps being taken to address the issue. This message must strike a balance between honesty and optimism, acknowledging the severity of the attack while assuring stakeholders of the organization's commitment to resolving the issue.

Identifying Key Stakeholders: A critical part of the communication strategy is identifying the key stakeholders who need to be informed. This includes employees, customers, partners, investors, and regulatory bodies. Each group may require a tailored message that addresses their specific concerns and interests. For instance, customers will be primarily concerned with the safety of their personal data and the restoration of services, while investors will be interested in the attack's impact on the company's financial health and reputation.

Choosing the Appropriate Channels: The next step is selecting the appropriate channels for communication. This can vary depending on the stakeholder group and the urgency of the message. Email and official statements on the company website may be suitable for detailed communications, while social media can be used for more immediate, brief updates. Internal communication tools such as intranets, team meetings, and direct emails are effective for keeping employees informed.

Ongoing Updates and Transparency: It's essential to provide ongoing updates as the recovery process progresses. Stakeholders appreciate transparency and being kept in the loop, even if the news isn't entirely positive. Regular updates can help manage expectations and reduce uncertainty, which is crucial for maintaining trust.

Feedback Mechanisms: Incorporating feedback mechanisms into the communication strategy allows stakeholders to voice their concerns and questions. This can be achieved through dedicated email addresses, hotlines, and social media engagement. Listening to stakeholders not only provides valuable insights into their concerns but also demonstrates the organization's commitment to addressing their needs.

Rebuilding Trust Through Action: Ultimately, the most effective way to communicate with stakeholders during recovery is through actions rather than words. Demonstrating a robust response to the attack, outlining the steps taken to prevent future incidents, and following through on recovery plans are vital. This includes transparently sharing any changes to policies, security enhancements, and lessons learned from the incident.

Post-Recovery Communication: Once services have been fully restored, a comprehensive post-recovery report should be shared with all stakeholders. This report should detail the attack, the steps taken during the recovery, the lessons learned, and the measures implemented to prevent future attacks. This final communication is an opportunity to close the incident on a note of resilience and readiness for the future.

Effective communication with stakeholders during the recovery from a DDoS attack is a multifaceted challenge that requires careful planning, empathy, and transparency. By following these guidelines, organizations can maintain and even strengthen their relationships with stakeholders, turning a moment of crisis into an opportunity to demonstrate resilience, competence, and integrity.

Ensuring Data Integrity and Preventing Data Loss

Immediate Measures for Data Protection: As soon as a DDoS attack is detected, immediate measures must be taken to secure data. This includes isolating affected systems to prevent the spread of potential malware or breaches that could accompany a DDoS attack. Implementing strict access controls and monitoring for unusual access patterns can also help secure data against unauthorized access during this vulnerable period.

Data Backup and Recovery Plans: A cornerstone of data integrity is a robust backup and recovery plan. Regularly updated backups, stored in multiple, geographically dispersed locations, can significantly mitigate the risk of data loss. Cloud-based backup solutions offer scalability and accessibility, but it's crucial to ensure these solutions themselves are secured against potential cyber threats. Testing these plans regularly through drills can ensure they are effective and can be executed swiftly in the wake of an attack.

Encryption and Data Masking: Encrypting data at rest and in transit can protect against unauthorized access. In the event that data is intercepted or accessed, encryption ensures that the information remains unintelligible without the decryption key. Similarly, data masking and tokenization can protect sensitive information such as personal identification numbers and financial details, rendering them useless to attackers.

Implementing a Secure Data Lifecycle: Managing the lifecycle of data—from creation, storage, use, to deletion—is critical in maintaining its integrity. Policies should define the duration for which data is retained, the secure storage methods, and the procedures for its safe deletion when no longer needed. This lifecycle approach ensures that data is protected at all stages and reduces the risk of data loss or leakage.

Real-time Monitoring and Anomaly Detection: Implementing real-time monitoring systems can provide early warnings of data integrity issues or potential data loss scenarios. Anomaly detection algorithms can identify unusual patterns that may indicate a cyber threat or system malfunction, allowing for immediate remediation actions to protect the data.

Employee Training and Awareness: Employees play a crucial role in maintaining data integrity. Regular training sessions on data protection best practices, recognizing phishing attempts, and secure handling of data can empower employees to act as a first line of defense against data loss and integrity threats.

Incident Response and Forensics: Post-attack, a detailed forensic analysis can help in understanding the attack vectors used and any potential data integrity compromises. An incident response team should assess the extent of any data corruption or loss, initiate recovery procedures from backups, and apply lessons learned to strengthen data protection measures.

Legal and Compliance Considerations: Ensuring data integrity and preventing loss also involves compliance with legal and regulatory requirements related to data protection. Organizations must stay informed about these requirements and integrate compliance measures into their data protection strategies.

Continuous Improvement: The threat landscape is constantly evolving, and so should an organization's data protection strategies. Regularly reviewing and updating data protection measures, in light of new threats and emerging technologies, is essential for ensuring long-term data integrity and security.

By implementing these strategies, organizations can significantly enhance their resilience against data integrity and loss challenges posed by DDoS attacks. Protecting data is not just about deploying the right technologies but also about fostering a culture of security awareness and preparedness across the organization.

Reviewing and Updating Policies

Initiating Policy Review: The first step in strengthening security postures following a DDoS attack involves a thorough audit of existing cybersecurity policies. This audit should assess the effectiveness of current procedures during the attack, identify any shortcomings, and highlight areas of improvement. The review process should be comprehensive, covering aspects such as incident response, data protection, employee training, and access controls.

Stakeholder Engagement: Updating cybersecurity policies is not a task that should be siloed within the IT department. It requires the active engagement of stakeholders from across the organization, including legal, human resources, operations, and executive leadership. This multidisciplinary approach ensures that policy updates are holistic and align with the broader organizational objectives and compliance requirements.

Incorporating Lessons Learned: An invaluable source of insights for policy updates comes from the lessons learned during and after the DDoS attack. These insights can reveal vulnerabilities in the network infrastructure, lapses in employee awareness, or inefficiencies in incident response protocols. By integrating these lessons into updated policies, organizations can close security gaps and enhance their defensive posture.

Adapting to Technological Advances: Cybersecurity is a field that is perpetually in flux, driven by rapid technological advancements. Policies must therefore be flexible enough to accommodate new security technologies and practices. Whether it's adopting next-generation firewalls, leveraging cloud-based DDoS mitigation services, or implementing advanced encryption standards, updated policies should reflect the latest in cybersecurity innovation.

Regulatory Compliance: The legal landscape surrounding data protection and cybersecurity is also constantly evolving. Policy updates must take into account any changes in legislation, ensuring that the organization remains in compliance with data protection laws, industry regulations, and national security standards. This is critical not only for safeguarding against cyber threats but also for avoiding legal and financial penalties.

Training and Awareness: Updated policies are only as effective as the people who implement them. A crucial component of the policy review process is the development and delivery of updated training programs for all employees. These programs should cover the latest cybersecurity threats, safe data handling practices, and the roles and responsibilities of employees in maintaining organizational security.

Continuous Monitoring and Review: Cybersecurity is not a 'set and forget' proposition. Even after policies have been updated, they must be continuously monitored for effectiveness and compliance. Regular security audits, penetration testing, and incident response drills can provide ongoing insights into the adequacy of policies and practices, prompting further updates as necessary.

Feedback Loops: Establishing mechanisms for feedback on security policies from employees can unearth practical challenges and innovative solutions that might not be apparent from a top-down perspective. This feedback loop can be instrumental in fine-tuning policies to make them more applicable and effective in the real world.

By systematically reviewing and updating policies in the aftermath of a DDoS attack, organizations can not only recover more effectively but also build a more robust and resilient cybersecurity framework. This proactive and iterative approach to policy management is crucial in navigating the complex and ever-changing cybersecurity landscape, ensuring that the organization is prepared to meet future challenges head-on.

The Need for Dynamic Security Policies

Building a Framework for Adaptation: The cornerstone of dynamic security policies is their inherent capacity for adaptation. This requires establishing a framework that supports rapid policy evolution in response to emerging threats and technological advancements. Such a framework might include protocols for regular policy reviews, threat intelligence monitoring, and the integration of agile methodologies into policy development processes.

Leveraging Threat Intelligence: Effective dynamic policies are informed by a continuous influx of threat intelligence. This intelligence feeds into the policy adaptation process, providing real-time insights into new DDoS attack vectors, threat actor tactics, and vulnerability disclosures. By integrating threat intelligence into the policy review cycle, organizations can ensure their defenses remain relevant and robust against the latest threats.

Predictive Policy Modeling: Beyond reactive adaptation, dynamic security policies embrace predictive modeling techniques to forecast future threat landscapes. Utilizing data analytics and machine learning algorithms, organizations can analyze trends in cyberattacks and predict potential future threats. This forward-looking approach allows for the preemptive strengthening of defenses before new threats materialize.

Cross-Functional Policy Development: Dynamic policies thrive on the diversity of perspectives. Their development should engage not just IT and cybersecurity teams, but also stakeholders from legal, compliance, operations, and other relevant departments. This cross-functional collaboration ensures that policies are well-rounded, comply with regulatory requirements, and resonate with the operational realities of the entire organization.

Engagement in Cybersecurity Communities: The fluid nature of cyber threats necessitates engagement with broader cybersecurity communities. Participation in industry forums, cybersecurity consortia, and threat sharing platforms can provide valuable external insights that inform dynamic policy adjustments. This collaborative approach enriches an organization's understanding of the cyber threat landscape and fosters a culture of continuous learning and adaptation.

Simulation and Testing: Dynamic security policies must be rigorously tested through simulations and red team exercises. These exercises should mimic the most current and challenging DDoS attack scenarios, providing a realistic assessment of the organization's preparedness and the effectiveness of its policies. Regular testing ensures that policies are not only theoretically sound but also practically effective.

Employee Training and Awareness: As policies evolve, so too must the training and awareness programs for employees. Continuous education on the latest cybersecurity practices, emerging threats, and policy changes is essential. This ensures that the human element of the organization's defenses remains vigilant and informed, capable of responding adeptly to any signs of a DDoS attack.

Feedback Mechanisms: Incorporating feedback mechanisms into the policy development process allows for the iterative refinement of policies based on operational feedback and post-incident analyses. This feedback, sourced from employees, security audits, and incident post-mortems, is invaluable for identifying policy gaps and areas for enhancement.

Dynamic security policies represent an organization's commitment to an ever-vigilant, adaptive stance in the face of the cyber threatscape. By fostering a culture that values continuous policy evolution, organizations can ensure they remain a step ahead of attackers, thereby safeguarding their digital assets and reputation in an increasingly hostile digital environment. Through strategic planning, cross-disciplinary collaboration, and a commitment to ongoing education and testing, the foundation for a resilient cyber future is built—one adaptive policy at a time.

Incorporating New Insights and Technologies into the DDOS Defense Plan

At the forefront of this revolution stands Artificial Intelligence (AI) and Machine Learning (ML). These technologies offer unparalleled agility in detecting and mitigating DDOS attacks. By analyzing patterns of network traffic in real time, AI algorithms can identify anomalies that signal an impending attack, often before it fully manifests. Furthermore, ML can learn from past attacks, continuously refining its understanding and enhancing its predictive capabilities. The integration of AI and ML into DDOS defense mechanisms represents a leap towards not merely reactive, but proactive defense strategies.

Quantum computing, with its promise of processing power magnitudes beyond current capabilities, presents a paradoxical scenario. On one hand, it heralds the potential for quantum-resistant encryption methods, offering a new layer of security against attacks. On the other, in the hands of adversaries, it could empower attackers with the ability to break traditional encryption, ushering in an era of quantum-level DDOS attacks. Preparing for this eventuality necessitates a radical rethinking of our encryption methodologies, ensuring they are quantum-resistant.

Blockchain technology, with its intrinsic characteristics of decentralization, transparency, and immutability, offers a novel approach to DDOS defense. By decentralizing DNS services and distributing data across a blockchain, we can significantly mitigate the risk of a single point of failure, a common target in DDOS attacks. Moreover, the transparent nature of blockchain ensures that any malicious alteration of data can be quickly identified and rectified, adding an additional layer of security against attack manipulation.

The proliferation of Internet of Things (IoT) devices introduces both vulnerabilities and opportunities in the context of DDOS attacks. On the vulnerability side, insecure IoT devices can be co-opted into botnets, serving as unwitting participants in massive DDOS attacks. However, on the opportunity side, properly secured IoT devices, equipped with the latest in endpoint security technologies, can serve as an extensive network of sentinels. These devices can monitor for unusual traffic patterns, providing an early warning system against potential attacks.

Incorporating new insights and technologies into our DDOS defense plans necessitates a culture of continuous learning and adaptation. Cybersecurity professionals must remain abreast of the latest developments in technology and threat vectors. This ongoing education, coupled with regular security audits and the implementation of adaptive security policies, forms the bedrock of a dynamic defense strategy that can evolve in tandem with the threats it seeks to neutralize.

Finally, the battle against DDOS attacks is not one to be fought in isolation. The sharing of threat intelligence among businesses, cybersecurity firms, and governmental agencies plays a pivotal role in fortifying our collective defenses. Through collaborative efforts and the establishment of shared protocols for threat detection and mitigation, we can build a more resilient digital ecosystem, one that is capable of withstanding the ever-evolving threats of the digital age.

incorporating new insights and technologies into DDOS defense plans is not merely an option; it is an imperative. As we continue to navigate the complexities of the digital landscape, our success in thwarting DDOS attacks will hinge on our ability to innovate, adapt, and unite in our efforts. The path forward is clear: by harnessing the power of emerging technologies and fostering a culture of continuous learning and collaboration, we can secure our digital future against the specter of DDOS attacks.

Regular Review Cycle for Security Measures and Policies

The foundation of a robust review cycle is the establishment of a baseline—a comprehensive audit of current security measures, policies, and their efficacy. This involves a meticulous examination of the existing security infrastructure, from firewalls and anti-DDOS protocols to employee awareness and response plans. The aim is to identify any vulnerabilities, outdated practices, or policies that may no longer align with the latest in cybersecurity best practices.

Cybersecurity is not the sole purview of the IT department; it is a multidisciplinary concern that spans the entire organization. Integrating insights from various departments—notably IT, operations, legal, and human resources—can provide a holistic view of the organization's defensive posture. This cross-pollination of perspectives is invaluable in identifying potential vulnerabilities and areas for improvement that may not be apparent from a purely technical standpoint.

Determining the frequency and timing of reviews is critical. Given the fast-paced evolution of cyber threats, a semi-annual review cycle is advisable at a minimum, with provisions for ad-hoc reviews in response to significant threats or security breaches. Timing the reviews to coincide with strategic planning sessions can ensure that cybersecurity remains a central consideration in organizational planning and resource allocation.

Each review cycle should include an assessment of emerging technologies, trends, and threat intelligence. This not only encompasses advancements in cybersecurity technologies but also an understanding of the evolving threat landscape, including new DDOS attack vectors. Participation in industry forums, cybersecurity consortia, and partnerships with cybersecurity firms can augment this intelligence, providing fresh insights and approaches to fortifying defenses.

The culmination of the review cycle is the revision of security measures and policies. This step must be approached with both deliberation and agility—deliberation to ensure that changes are thoughtful and data-driven, and agility to implement these revisions swiftly to stay ahead of potential threats. Revised policies should be disseminated promptly to all stakeholders, accompanied by training sessions where necessary to ensure that all personnel are up-to-date on the latest protocols and practices.

Finally, the regular review cycle should be viewed as an iterative process of continuous improvement. Each cycle builds on the learnings of the previous, adapting not only to changes in the threat landscape but also to technological advancements and shifts in organizational structure and priorities. This approach ensures that cybersecurity measures and policies remain dynamic, evolving in lockstep with both external threats and internal developments.

instituting a regular review cycle for security measures and policies is indispensable in the current climate of heightened cyber threats. It ensures that an organization's defenses are not only robust but also adaptive, capable of responding to the ever-changing tactics of adversaries. By embracing a disciplined, inclusive, and forward-looking approach to these reviews, organizations can significantly enhance their resilience against DDOS attacks, safeguarding their assets, reputation, and the trust of their stakeholders.

CHAPTER 8: INNOVATIONS IN DDOS DEFENSE

At the forefront of this technological vanguard are Artificial Intelligence (AI) and Machine Learning (ML). These technologies offer unprecedented capabilities in detecting and responding to DDoS attacks in real-time. AI and ML algorithms can analyze vast swathes of network data, identifying patterns and anomalies that hint at a nascent DDoS attack. This predictive capability enables preemptive action, thwarting attackers before they can inflict damage. Moreover, as these systems are exposed to more data, their detection capabilities become increasingly refined, learning from each attack to bolster defenses against future threats.

Blockchain technology, best known for underpinning cryptocurrencies, holds promising applications in cybersecurity. Its decentralized nature can offer a robust solution to securing the integrity of communication between devices in a network. By leveraging blockchain, networks can ensure that data has not been tampered with, adding an extra layer of security against DDoS attacks that rely on intercepting and altering data packets. Furthermore, blockchain can facilitate a new model of decentralized DNS, mitigating the risk of DDoS attacks aimed at disrupting central DNS providers.

Quantum computing presents a paradox in the realm of cybersecurity. On one hand, its potential to break traditional encryption methods could render existing security protocols obsolete, offering attackers a powerful tool. On the other, quantum encryption promises to create secure communications that are theoretically impervious to interception or decryption, including by quantum computers themselves. The race is on to harness quantum computing for defense, developing quantum-resistant encryption methods before attackers can exploit it for offensive purposes.

The proliferation of IoT devices introduces a multitude of vectors for DDoS attacks, with many devices lacking adequate security measures. Emerging technologies focus on "Security by Design" principles for IoT devices, embedding robust security features at the manufacturing stage. This includes secure boot mechanisms, encrypted communications, and the ability to receive regular security updates. By fortifying the weakest links in the network, the overall resilience against DDoS attacks is significantly enhanced.

NFV and SDN are transforming traditional network architectures, offering flexible and dynamic network management. In the context of DDoS defense, these technologies enable the swift reallocation of network resources, rerouting traffic away from targeted services to mitigate the impact of an attack. Furthermore, they facilitate the deployment of virtual DDoS defense mechanisms that can be scaled on demand, providing robust protection tailored to the attack's intensity and sophistication.

The future of DDoS defense also lies in collaborative efforts, leveraging shared threat intelligence and coordinated response strategies. Emerging platforms and frameworks facilitate real-time sharing of threat data among organizations, enhancing collective defense capabilities. By unifying efforts, the cybersecurity community can present a united front against attackers, significantly diminishing the efficacy of DDoS campaigns.

the landscape of DDoS defense is undergoing a radical transformation, driven by the advent of groundbreaking technologies. These innovations not only elevate the sophistication of cybersecurity measures but also redefine the strategic approach to defending against DDoS attacks. As we venture into this new era, the fusion of AI, blockchain, quantum computing, and collaborative defense mechanisms heralds a promising horizon for cybersecurity, promising a future where DDoS attacks are not just mitigated but preemptively neutralized.

Advancements in AI and Machine Learning for DDOS Detection and Response

The application of ML in DDoS defense primarily revolves around anomaly detection models. These models are trained on vast datasets comprising normal network traffic patterns, enabling them to distinguish between legitimate traffic and potential threats with remarkable accuracy. Anomaly detection algorithms, such as clustering, neural networks, and decision trees, are employed to scrutinize real-time data flows, identifying deviations that may signify a DDoS attack. This capability allows for the early detection of attacks, often before they can cause significant disruption, and facilitates swift defensive reactions.

Predictive analytics harnesses AI's power to analyze historical data and predict future attack patterns. By understanding the characteristics of past DDoS attacks, AI algorithms can forecast potential vulnerabilities and likely targets within the network. This foresight enables administrators to reinforce defenses proactively, placing resources where they are most needed to thwart impending attacks. Furthermore, predictive analytics can offer insights into the evolving tactics employed by cybercriminals, allowing for the continuous refinement of defense strategies.

One of the most critical advancements in leveraging AI and ML against DDoS attacks is the development of automated response systems. These systems can instantaneously take countermeasures against an attack, significantly reducing the time between detection and response. Automated responses can include the redirection of traffic, the deployment of additional firewall rules, or the activation of rate-limiting protocols, among others. The autonomy of these systems in making real-time decisions is crucial in mitigating the impact of DDoS attacks, particularly those of high volume or sophistication.

For AI and ML technologies to be effective in DDoS defense, they must be seamlessly integrated into existing cybersecurity frameworks. This integration involves the deployment of AI-driven security appliances and software solutions within the network infrastructure, as well as the adoption of AI-based security information and event management (SIEM) systems. Such integration not only enhances the detection and response capabilities but also improves overall security posture through insights generated by AI analysis, contributing to a more robust and resilient network.

While the advancements in AI and ML offer promising

solutions for DDoS defense, they are not without challenges. The accuracy of ML models depends on the quality and quantity of the training data, requiring continuous updates to adapt to new attack vectors. Additionally, there is the risk of adversarial AI, where attackers use AI techniques to evade detection. Addressing these challenges necessitates ongoing research and development, with future directions focusing on the creation of adversarial-resistant models, the exploration of unsupervised learning techniques for anomaly detection, and the development of more sophisticated predictive analytics tools.

the advancements in AI and ML are pivotal in the development of dynamic and effective defenses against DDoS attacks. By leveraging these technologies, cybersecurity professionals can enhance their detection capabilities, automate their response strategies, and anticipate future threats, thereby mitigating the impact of DDoS attacks and securing the digital infrastructure against this ever-evolving threat. The continuous innovation in AI and ML technologies remains a beacon of hope in the relentless battle against cyber aggression, promising a future where networks are not only defended but also intelligently adapted to counteract the DDoS threat landscape.

The Potential of Blockchain for Enhancing Network Security

blockchain is a distributed ledger technology that ensures the integrity and transparency of a data exchange without the need for a central authority. Each block in the chain contains a number of transactions; every time a new transaction occurs on the blockchain, a record of that transaction is added to every participant's ledger. This decentralization is pivotal for network security, as it removes single points of failure that hackers can exploit.

Blockchain's architecture inherently guards against data tampering. Once a transaction is entered into the ledger and the subsequent blocks are added, altering the transaction becomes computationally impractical. This immutable record-keeping is vital for maintaining data integrity, ensuring that any unauthorized attempts to modify data can be easily detected and traced back. Furthermore, cryptographic techniques ensure the confidentiality of the transactions, allowing participants to verify the authenticity of information without exposing the actual data.

The decentralized nature of blockchain can be leveraged to create more resilient networks. By distributing data across a network of nodes, blockchain mitigates the risk of centralized repositories becoming targets for DDoS attacks. This dispersal not only makes it exceedingly difficult for attackers to pinpoint and compromise specific data points but also ensures that the network remains operational even if some nodes are under attack or malfunction.

Blockchain introduces the concept of smart contracts: self-executing contracts with the terms directly written into code. These can be designed to enforce security policies automatically. For instance, if a network anomaly indicative of a DDoS attack is detected, a smart contract could automatically redistribute network traffic or adjust firewalls to mitigate the attack without human intervention. This rapid, rule-based response can significantly reduce the window of vulnerability during cyber attacks.

While blockchain holds significant promise for enhancing network security, its implementation is not without challenges. The technology's nascent state means that standards and best practices are still evolving. There are also concerns regarding the scalability of blockchain solutions and the computational resources required to maintain the ledger, which could impact network performance. Furthermore, the effectiveness of blockchain-based security relies on the strength of the underlying cryptographic methods and the security of the network nodes themselves.

As blockchain technology matures, its potential applications in network security are vast. Looking ahead, we could see blockchain being used to create verifiable logs of network activity, secure messaging systems, and decentralized identity verification systems, among others. These applications could significantly enhance the ability to detect, prevent, and respond to cyber threats, marking a new era in network security.

In sum, the intersection of blockchain technology and network security opens up exciting avenues for protecting digital infrastructures. By capitalizing on blockchain's decentralization, immutability, and cryptographic security, it is possible to envisage a future where networks are not only more resistant to cyber attacks but are also self-healing and adaptive. While challenges remain, the ongoing advancements in blockchain technology are a beacon of hope, offering novel solutions to age-old security problems and paving the way for a more secure and trustworthy digital landscape.

Future Trends in Cybersecurity That Could Reshape DDOS Defense

Quantum computing holds the promise of processing capabilities far beyond what current digital computers can achieve. Its potential to crack complex cryptographic algorithms that currently secure the internet is both a boon and a bane. On the one hand, quantum computing could render traditional encryption methods obsolete, potentially opening the floodgates to unprecedented cyber threats. On the other hand, it harbors the potential for quantum encryption—offering a level of security that is theoretically unbreakable. Quantum-resistant algorithms are being developed, aiming to fortify networks against the quantum computing era, ensuring that DDoS defense mechanisms remain impenetrable.

Artificial Intelligence (AI) and Machine Learning (ML) are at the forefront of transforming cybersecurity strategies from reactive to proactive stances. Predictive cybersecurity leverages AI and ML to analyze patterns, detect anomalies, and predict potential threats before they materialize. This paradigm shift could dramatically enhance DDoS defense mechanisms by enabling real-time detection and neutralization of threats, minimizing damage. AI-driven systems could automatically adjust security postures based on the evolving threat landscape, ensuring optimal protection against DDoS attacks with minimal human intervention.

Edge computing decentralizes data processing, pushing it closer to the source of data generation. This model contrasts with traditional cloud computing, where data is processed in centralized data centers. By distributing data across numerous edge nodes, the attack surface for DDoS attacks is significantly expanded, complicating the efforts of attackers. Furthermore, edge computing can reduce latency in DDoS detection and response, enhancing the ability to thwart attacks swiftly. As edge computing gains traction, developing DDoS defense strategies that leverage this distributed architecture will be paramount.

As explored in the previous section, blockchain technology harbors significant potential for enhancing network security. Beyond its current applications, future blockchain innovations could further redefine DDoS defense. For instance, decentralized DNS systems based on blockchain could mitigate the risk of DNS-based DDoS attacks. Additionally, blockchain could facilitate secure, decentralized sharing of threat intelligence, enabling a collaborative approach to DDoS defense among organizations worldwide.

The Zero Trust security model, predicated on the principle of "never trust, always verify," is gaining momentum. In the context of DDoS defense, Zero Trust architecture can minimize the potential impact of attacks by strictly limiting access to network resources and rigorously verifying all access requests, regardless of their origin. This approach not only enhances security posture but also ensures that, even in the event of a DDoS attack, the integrity and availability of critical resources are preserved.

The future of cybersecurity, particularly in defending against DDoS attacks, lies in collaboration. Public-private partnerships, sharing of threat intelligence among competitors, and global cybersecurity alliances are emerging trends. These collaborative efforts aim to pool resources, knowledge, and capabilities to combat cyber threats more effectively. By sharing real-time threat intelligence and coordinating defense strategies, the global cybersecurity community can present a united front against DDoS attackers.

the future of DDoS defense is poised at the intersection of cutting-edge technologies and collaborative paradigms. From quantum-resistant encryption and AI-powered predictive cybersecurity to the adoption of Zero Trust architecture and the exploration of blockchain's full potential, these trends offer a glimpse into a future where digital defenses are as dynamic and sophisticated as the threats they aim to counter. As the cybersecurity community embraces these innovations, the resilience of networks against DDoS attacks will not only improve but also transform the digital battlefield, ensuring a more secure and trustworthy cyber ecosystem.

Building a Proactive Defense Strategy Against DDoS Attacks

The cornerstone of a proactive defense strategy is the prioritization of threat intelligence. By harnessing real-time data on emerging threats, organizations can stay one step ahead of potential attackers. Investing in advanced threat intelligence platforms enables the identification of precursors to DDoS attacks, such as unusual traffic patterns or reconnaissance activities by attackers. This intelligence is not just reactive but predictive, offering insights into how and where attacks might occur, thereby facilitating preemptive measures.

Visibility is the lens through which the vast and complex digital environment of an organization is understood. Enhanced network visibility allows for the detection of anomalies that could signify an impending DDoS attack. This includes monitoring incoming traffic to identify surges that deviate from baseline levels, which could indicate a DDoS in progress. Employing sophisticated monitoring tools that utilize machine learning algorithms can automate the detection process, ensuring rapid response to threats.

The concept of adaptability is critical in the realm of cybersecurity. An adaptive security architecture is designed to evolve in response to the changing threat landscape. This involves the integration of advanced security technologies such as behavioural analytics, which assesses user and system behaviours to detect deviations indicative of a DDoS attack. Furthermore, the architecture should be agile, enabling quick modifications to security policies and configurations to counter new and emerging threats effectively.

A proactive defense strategy extends beyond technological solutions; it encompasses the people within the organization. Cultivating a culture of cybersecurity awareness through regular training and education programs ensures that every member of the organization understands their role in protecting against DDoS attacks. This human-centric approach is pivotal, as human error or oversight can often be exploited by attackers to launch a DDoS attack.

The battle against DDoS attacks is not fought in isolation. Collaboration and information sharing among businesses, cybersecurity experts, and government agencies can significantly bolster the collective defense against DDoS threats. Participating in cybersecurity forums, alliances, and consortiums allows for the exchange of threat intelligence and best practices, enhancing the ability to preempt and respond to DDoS attacks on a global scale.

A proactive defense strategy is iterative; it requires constant review and testing to ensure its efficacy. Conducting regular simulations of DDoS attacks provides valuable insights into the responsiveness and resilience of the current defense mechanisms. These exercises help identify vulnerabilities and areas for improvement, guiding the optimization of the defense strategy over time.

The scalability and flexibility of cloud-based DDoS mitigation services make them an integral component of a proactive defense strategy. These services can absorb and disperse the massive volumes of traffic generated in a DDoS attack, protecting the organization's infrastructure. Moreover, cloud providers continually update their defenses against the latest

DDoS tactics, offering a layer of protection that evolves in tandem with the threat landscape.

building a proactive defense strategy against DDoS attacks is a multifaceted endeavor that necessitates a comprehensive approach. By prioritizing threat intelligence, enhancing network visibility, implementing adaptive security architectures, fostering a culture of cybersecurity awareness, collaborating with the broader cybersecurity community, regularly reviewing defense mechanisms, and leveraging cloud-based services, organizations can establish a dynamic and resilient defense posture. This strategy not only mitigates the impact of DDoS attacks but also empowers organizations to navigate the complexities of the digital age with confidence and security.

Moving from Reactive to Proactive Defense Mechanisms in DDoS Strategy

A proactive defense approach lies strategic planning and the anticipation of potential threats. This involves conducting comprehensive risk assessments to identify the most vulnerable elements of an organization's network infrastructure. With this insight, organizations can develop a layered defense strategy that addresses these vulnerabilities before they can be exploited in a DDoS attack.

The use of predictive analytics is pivotal in moving towards a proactive defense posture. By analyzing patterns and trends in network traffic, predictive analytics tools can identify irregularities that may signal an impending DDoS attack. This advanced warning system allows organizations to bolster their defenses in anticipation of an attack, rather than scrambling to respond once the attack is underway.

Machine learning algorithms represent a cornerstone technology in early detection efforts. These algorithms can continuously learn from network behavior, enabling them to detect the subtle signs of a DDoS attack in its nascent stages. By identifying these early indicators, organizations can initiate defensive protocols automatically, thereby mitigating the impact of the attack or averting it altogether.

Automation plays a crucial role in transitioning from reactive to proactive defense mechanisms. Automated security systems can instantaneously respond to potential threats, implementing predefined defense measures without the need for human intervention. This rapid response capability is essential for addressing the high-speed nature of DDoS attacks, where even a slight delay can result in significant damage.

Proactive defense is not a set-it-and-forget-it solution; it requires a commitment to continuous improvement and adaptation. This entails regular updates to security protocols, based on the latest threat intelligence and the evolving tactics of cyber attackers. Additionally, post-attack analyses should be conducted following any DDoS event, even if the attack was successfully mitigated. These analyses provide valuable lessons that can be used to further refine and strengthen defense strategies.

The complexity and scale of DDoS attacks often exceed the capabilities of any single organization. As such, moving towards proactive defense mechanisms involves participating in collaborative security initiatives. By sharing threat intelligence and pooling resources, organizations can collectively develop more robust defense mechanisms against DDoS attacks. These collaborative efforts extend to partnerships with internet service providers (ISPs) and cloud service providers, who play a critical role in implementing widespread defensive measures against DDoS traffic.

Finally, the shift towards proactive defense mechanisms must be supported by an ongoing effort to educate and empower all stakeholders. This includes not only IT professionals but also employees at every level of the organization. Through regular training sessions and awareness programs, stakeholders can learn to recognize the early signs of a DDoS attack and understand their role in the organization's defense strategy.

moving from reactive to proactive defense mechanisms against DDoS attacks requires a comprehensive and multifaceted approach. By embracing strategic planning, predictive analytics, machine learning, automation, continuous improvement, collaborative security initiatives, and stakeholder education, organizations can develop a proactive defense posture that not only addresses the DDoS threats of today but also anticipates the challenges of tomorrow. This proactive stance empowers organizations to defend their digital assets more effectively, ensuring business continuity and the protection of sensitive information in an increasingly hostile cyber landscape.

The Importance of Threat Intelligence Sharing in DDoS Defense

Threat intelligence sharing serves as a catalyst for collective cyber resilience among organizations, industries, and nations. By pooling resources and information, entities can achieve a more comprehensive understanding of the DDoS threat landscape. This collective insight enables participants to identify and mitigate potential threats before they can escalate into full-blown attacks, thereby enhancing the overall security posture of all involved parties.

Effective threat intelligence sharing relies on robust mechanisms that facilitate the exchange of information in real-time. This includes the establishment of Information Sharing and Analysis Centers (ISACs), which serve specific sectors by collecting, analyzing, and disseminating critical cyber threat information among member organizations. Furthermore, automated threat intelligence platforms allow for the instant sharing of indicators of compromise (IoCs) and tactics, techniques, and procedures (TTPs) used by cyber attackers, enabling proactive defensive measures.

Despite its evident benefits, the path to effective threat intelligence sharing is fraught with challenges. Concerns over privacy, data protection, and the potential for competitive disadvantage often hinder the willingness of organizations to share sensitive information. Overcoming these challenges requires the establishment of trusted relationships, adherence to legal and regulatory frameworks, and the use of anonymized data sharing methods to protect sensitive information while still contributing to the collective defense effort.

Cultivating a culture of collaboration is fundamental to the success of threat intelligence sharing initiatives. This involves fostering an environment where sharing is recognized as a contribution to the greater good, rather than a loss of competitive edge. Education and awareness programs can play a critical role in changing mindsets, highlighting the mutual benefits of collaboration in enhancing cybersecurity.

Government and regulatory bodies have a crucial role to play in promoting threat intelligence sharing. By enacting policies that encourage or require information sharing within and across industries, and by providing platforms for such exchanges, these bodies can significantly enhance the collective ability to defend against DDoS and other cyber threats.

In the realm of DDoS defense, the sharing of threat intelligence enables organizations to gain early warnings about emerging attack trends, including new DDoS techniques and previously unknown vulnerabilities. Armed with this information, organizations can better tailor their defensive strategies, fortify their network infrastructures, and deploy targeted mitigation measures in anticipation of potential attacks.

The importance of threat intelligence sharing in the context of DDoS defense cannot be overstated. As cyber attackers continue to evolve and adapt, the collective sharing of knowledge and strategies among organizations, sectors, and nations becomes an invaluable weapon in the cybersecurity arsenal. By overcoming the challenges to effective sharing and fostering a culture of collaboration, the global community can enhance its resilience against the ever-present threat of DDoS attacks, safeguarding the integrity of our digital world for the future.

Strategies for Staying Ahead of DDoS Attackers

A foundational strategy in preempting DDoS attacks involves the implementation of proactive monitoring and anomaly detection systems. By continuously analyzing network traffic patterns and identifying deviations from the norm, organizations can detect the early signs of a DDoS attack. Advanced machine learning algorithms and artificial intelligence (AI) technologies enhance the precision of detection methods, enabling the differentiation between legitimate traffic spikes and malicious DDoS traffic.

To mitigate the volume of malicious requests during a DDoS attack, organizations can deploy advanced filtering solutions.

These technologies work by scrutinizing incoming traffic to the network and filtering out suspect or malicious data packets based on predefined criteria, such as IP reputation, geolocation data, and traffic patterns. Employing such filters at the network perimeter serves as a first line of defense, reducing the attack surface available to cybercriminals.

Designing a resilient network architecture is paramount in defending against DDoS attacks. Strategies include the decentralization of resources across multiple data centers, the adoption of cloud-based services capable of absorbing high traffic volumes, and the implementation of redundant systems to ensure service continuity. By dispersing network assets, organizations can dilute the impact of an attack, preventing attackers from incapacitating critical services with a single strike.

Cloud-based DDoS mitigation services offer scalable, on-demand resources to counteract the surge in traffic during an attack. These services can rapidly absorb and diffuse DDoS attacks, drawing upon their extensive global infrastructure. Moreover, cloud providers continually update their defense mechanisms in response to emerging threats, affording organizations with up-to-date protection without the need for significant capital investment in on-premises hardware.

Beyond technical defenses, preparing a comprehensive incident response plan is crucial for minimizing the impact of DDoS attacks. This plan should outline the steps to be taken in the event of an attack, including internal and external communication protocols, procedures for traffic rerouting, and mechanisms for incident analysis and reporting. Regular training and simulation exercises can ensure that all stakeholders are prepared to execute the plan efficiently under real-world conditions.

In the fight against DDoS attackers, there is strength in numbers. Engaging in collaboration networks and information-sharing platforms allows organizations to exchange insights on emerging DDoS trends, tactics, and effective countermeasures. This collective intelligence can significantly enhance the ability of individual organizations to anticipate and respond to attacks, fostering a more resilient digital ecosystem.

Lastly, investing in cybersecurity education and awareness programs for staff can fortify an organization's human firewall. Educating employees about the signs of a DDoS attack and proper security protocols can prevent inadvertent actions that may exacerbate the situation. A well-informed workforce is a critical asset in maintaining an organization's cybersecurity posture.

As DDoS attackers continually evolve their tactics, organizations must adopt a multifaceted and proactive approach to defense. By leveraging advanced technologies, fostering resilient network infrastructures, preparing comprehensive response strategies, and promoting collaboration and education, organizations can position themselves to stay ahead of DDoS attackers. This proactive stance not only mitigates the risk of attacks but also ensures that the organization can rapidly recover, maintaining service availability and integrity in the face of evolving cyber threats.

Anticipating Future DDoS Threats

The continuous evolution of technology serves as a double-edged sword in the realm of cybersecurity. On one hand, advancements in computing power, artificial intelligence (AI), and the Internet of Things (IoT) offer promising new avenues for defending against cyber threats. On the other, these same technologies provide cybercriminals with sophisticated tools to orchestrate more potent and complex DDoS attacks. For instance, the proliferation of IoT devices introduces a vast array of insecure endpoints that can be co-opted into botnets, significantly amplifying the scale and impact of attacks.

AI and machine learning (ML) technologies hold the potential to revolutionize DDoS attacks. Cybercriminals could leverage AI to automate the process of finding and exploiting vulnerabilities, optimizing attack strategies in real-time, and circumventing traditional defense mechanisms. AI-driven DDoS attacks could dynamically adjust their tactics based on the observed response from targeted systems, making them more difficult to predict and mitigate.

The anticipated advent of quantum computing promises to deliver computational capabilities far beyond the reach of today's systems. Among its potential impacts is the ability to break current cryptographic defenses, rendering many of today's security protocols obsolete. While the widespread availability of quantum computers may still be years away, the threat they pose to cybersecurity, including the facilitation of unprecedented DDoS attacks, cannot be ignored.

To stay ahead of these emerging threats, organizations must adopt a proactive and adaptive cybersecurity posture. This involves investing in research and development to understand the potential applications of new technologies for both defense and offense in cyberspace. Developing quantum-resistant cryptographic protocols, enhancing the security of IoT devices, and leveraging AI for defense are all critical steps in future-proofing against DDoS threats.

Moreover, building flexible and resilient network infrastructures that can withstand or quickly recover from attacks will be essential. This may include the use of decentralized systems, blockchain technology for enhanced security and transparency, and cloud-based solutions for scalable defense capabilities.

The complexity and global nature of future DDoS threats necessitate a collaborative approach to cybersecurity. Governments, private sector entities, and international organizations must work together to establish norms and regulations that promote cyber hygiene, facilitate information sharing, and foster the development of global cybersecurity talents. Joint efforts in threat intelligence sharing and coordinated response strategies can significantly enhance collective defense capabilities against DDoS attacks.

Anticipating future DDoS threats requires a multifaceted approach, embracing technological innovation, strategic planning, and international cooperation. By understanding the potential directions from which future threats may emerge and adopting a proactive stance, the cybersecurity community can not only defend against these evolving challenges but also contribute to a more secure and resilient digital world.

Predicting the Evolution of DDOS Attack Vectors

The digital landscape is akin to a vast ocean, constantly shifting under the influence of technological innovation and the cunning of cyber adversaries. As we navigate these turbulent waters, our foresight into the evolution of Distributed Denial of Service (DDoS) attack vectors becomes not just a matter of intellectual curiosity but a crucial linchpin in our collective cybersecurity defenses.

Historically, DDoS attacks have evolved from mere annoyances carried out by script kiddies seeking notoriety, to sophisticated onslaughts orchestrated by well-funded, highly organized cybercriminal entities. These entities leverage DDoS as a smokescreen for more sinister activities, or as a form of cyber warfare aimed at crippling national infrastructure, disrupting economic activities, or influencing political processes.

The nexus of DDoS evolution is closely tied to the proliferation of emerging technologies. The Internet of Things (IoT), with its legion of poorly secured devices, presents a formidable army awaiting conscription by botnet herders. The sheer volume and diversity of these devices provide a fertile ground for amplifying the scale and complexity of DDoS attacks.

Moreover, advancements in cloud computing, while offering scalability and resilience to businesses, also usher in novel attack vectors. Misconfigured cloud resources can be hijacked to launch potent DDoS attacks, exploiting the vast computational resources at their disposal. Additionally, the adoption of 5G technology promises to increase the speed and reduce the latency of internet communications, which, paradoxically, could serve to enhance both the efficacy of DDoS mitigation strategies and the devastating potential of the attacks themselves.

Predicting the future trajectory of DDoS attack vectors reveals a marked shift towards multi-vector strategies. These strategies combine volumetric attacks, aimed at overwhelming bandwidth, with application-layer attacks that cripple specific server resources or applications, and state-exhaustion attacks targeting firewalls and load balancers. By diversifying their tactics, attackers can circumvent traditional defense mechanisms, complicating mitigation efforts and increasing the likelihood of success.

Furthermore, the advent of AI and machine learning technologies heralds a new era where DDoS attacks could be dynamically adjusted in real-time, responding to mitigation efforts with alarming agility. AI-driven botnets might analyze traffic in real-time, devising and executing attack patterns that evolve to exploit detected vulnerabilities or to avoid detection altogether.

The democratization of cybercrime, facilitated by the Cybercrime-as-a-Service (CaaS) model, lowers the entry barrier for launching sophisticated DDoS attacks. With DDoS toolkits and botnet rentals readily available on dark web marketplaces, the pool of potential attackers is no longer confined to technical experts. This commoditization of DDoS capabilities implies that the future landscape will likely see an increase in the frequency and diversity of attacks, launched by a broader cohort of adversaries with varying motives.

As we gaze into the horizon, the evolving nature of DDoS attack vectors underscores the imperative for robust, adaptive cybersecurity strategies. It's a clarion call for the cybersecurity community to foster innovation in defense mechanisms, to cultivate a proactive security posture, and to bolster collaborative efforts across industries and borders. The path forward demands a harmonized approach, leveraging advanced technologies, threat intelligence sharing, and continuous education to stay ahead of the curve.

Predicting the evolution of DDoS attacks is akin to charting a course through uncharted waters, requiring vigilance, adaptability, and the collective will to navigate the challenges that lie ahead. In this journey, our resilience, ingenuity, and unity become our beacon of hope, guiding us toward a secure digital future.

The Changing Landscape of Cyber Warfare and Its Impact on Cybersecurity

As the digital era progresses, the fabric of cyber warfare is undergoing a profound transformation, reshaping the battlefield on which nations, corporations, and individuals find themselves defending against an ever-evolving threat matrix. This metamorphosis is not only altering the tactics and tools of cyber adversaries but also significantly influencing the strategies underpinning cybersecurity defenses.

In recent years, the delineation between cybercriminal activities and state-sponsored cyber operations has blurred, with nations leveraging cyber capabilities to achieve strategic objectives. This melding of motives and methodologies has introduced a complexity into the cybersecurity domain, necessitating a recalibration of defense postures. State-sponsored actors, equipped with vast resources and advanced technological prowess, embark on campaigns that span espionage, intellectual property theft, and direct attacks on critical infrastructure. These campaigns often exhibit sophisticated levels of obfuscation and persistence, challenging traditional cybersecurity mechanisms to adapt.

The advent of Artificial Intelligence (AI) in cyber warfare represents a double-edged sword. On one hand, AI and machine learning algorithms offer promising advancements in threat detection and response, providing the ability to analyze vast datasets for identifying anomalous patterns indicative of a cyber attack. On the other hand, adversaries exploit these same technologies to automate attack processes, evolve attack strategies in real-time, and develop malware that eludes detection by learning from past cyber defense measures. This technological arms race signifies a pivotal shift in cyber warfare, compelling cybersecurity professionals to remain at the forefront of innovation to counteract AI-driven threats.

The impending arrival of quantum computing heralds a potential seismic shift in the cybersecurity landscape. Quantum computers, with their ability to solve complex problems at unprecedented speeds, pose a significant threat to the backbone of cybersecurity: encryption. Current encryption algorithms, once considered unassailable, may become vulnerable, exposing sensitive data to interception and decryption by quantum-enabled adversaries. This scenario underscores the urgency for quantum-resistant cryptographic standards, ensuring that cybersecurity infrastructures can withstand the quantum computing era.

The proliferation of Internet of Things (IoT) devices exponentially expands the cyber attack surface, offering new vectors for exploitation. From consumer gadgets to industrial control systems, the ubiquitous nature of connected devices presents a formidable challenge for cybersecurity defenses. The heterogeneity and often inadequate security measures of IoT devices create vulnerabilities that can be exploited for launching large-scale DDoS attacks, infiltrating networks, and compromising critical systems. In response, cybersecurity strategies are evolving to encompass not only the protection of traditional IT assets but also the safeguarding of this vast array of connected devices.

In the face of the changing landscape of cyber warfare, the concept of cyber resilience has emerged as a critical tenet of cybersecurity. Beyond mere prevention and defense, cyber resilience emphasizes the ability to withstand, rapidly recover from, and adapt to cyber attacks. This holistic approach involves a spectrum of strategies including robust incident response plans, comprehensive disaster recovery protocols, and continuous security posture assessments. It also entails a cultural shift within organizations, fostering awareness and preparedness across all levels of the workforce.

As the landscape of cyber warfare continues to evolve, it poses challenges that are complex, multifaceted, and global in scope. The impact on cybersecurity is profound, driving a perpetual cycle of adaptation and innovation. In this context, vigilance and collaboration emerge as foundational pillars. Establishing strong alliances among nations, industries, and the cybersecurity community will be paramount in sharing threat intelligence, developing best practices, and coordinating responses to emergent threats. Through united efforts and a commitment to innovation, the cybersecurity community can aspire to not just navigate but thrive in the turbulent waters of the digital age, safeguarding our collective digital future.

The Role of IoT Devices in the Future of DDOS Attacks

The exponential growth of IoT devices has irreversibly expanded the digital attack surface. Unlike traditional computing devices, many IoT devices are designed with minimal security features, making them susceptible to hijacking by malicious actors. These compromised devices can be corralled into vast botnets, orchestrating synchronized requests to overwhelm and incapacitate targeted servers or networks. The Mirai botnet incident serves as a stark reminder of the destructive potential inherent in unsecured IoT devices, signaling a pressing need for enhanced security protocols.

Addressing the security vulnerabilities of IoT devices presents a multifaceted challenge. First, the sheer diversity and volume of these devices create a logistical nightmare for implementing uniform security measures. Additionally, many IoT devices operate on proprietary systems with limited processing capabilities, restricting the deployment of conventional cybersecurity software. Furthermore, the lifespan of IoT devices often exceeds that of their support or update cycles, resulting in a growing number of devices with outdated security measures— a phenomenon known as "orphaned technology."

Future DDoS attacks leveraging IoT devices are likely to exhibit unprecedented sophistication and scale. With advancements in artificial intelligence and machine learning, malicious actors could orchestrate attacks that dynamically adjust tactics in real-time, targeting vulnerabilities as they emerge. Moreover, the integration of IoT devices across various sectors, including critical infrastructure, amplifies the potential impact of such attacks, raising significant concerns for national security and public safety.

Mitigating the threat of IoT-driven DDoS attacks necessitates a collaborative effort across stakeholders, including device manufacturers, regulatory bodies, and end-users. Key strategies include the development and enforcement of stringent security standards for IoT devices, fostering public awareness regarding IoT security practices, and deploying advanced threat detection and mitigation technologies. Additionally, leveraging blockchain technology could offer a decentralized approach to securing IoT devices, ensuring transparency and integrity in device communication and authentication.

As the role of IoT devices in DDoS attacks continues to evolve, adopting a proactive security posture is imperative. This entails continuous monitoring of IoT devices for signs of compromise, regular security audits, and the readiness to respond swiftly to potential threats. Moreover, fostering a culture of security within organizations can empower individuals to recognize and mitigate risks associated with IoT devices.

the role of IoT devices in the future of DDoS attacks underscores a critical juncture in cybersecurity. As we navigate this complex threat landscape, the collective efforts of the global cybersecurity community are paramount in developing resilient defenses against the looming specter of IoT-driven DDoS attacks. By embracing innovation, collaboration, and a proactive security mindset, we can fortify our digital world against the challenges that lie ahead, securing our interconnected future against the ever-evolving threats of cyber warfare.

Training and Education

In the ever-evolving battlefield of cyber security, one of the most effective weapons against DDoS attacks is comprehensive, continuous training and education. As the sophistication of DDoS strategies escalates, paralleled by the burgeoning role of IoT devices in these attacks, the imperative for robust cyber education has never been clearer. This segment explores the critical importance of cybersecurity education and training, not merely as a preventative measure, but as an indispensable component of a proactive defense strategy.

The realm of cybersecurity is dynamic, with new threats and vulnerabilities emerging at a breakneck pace. This constant evolution demands a commitment to continuous learning from those tasked with defending digital assets. Cybersecurity training programs, both formal and informal, serve as the crucible where the latest defensive tactics are forged and refined.

These programs must not only cover the technical aspects of security but also foster an understanding of the psychological and strategic underpinnings of cyber attacks.

For individuals at the outset of their cybersecurity journey, the path from novice to expert can seem daunting. Here, structured education programs, offering certifications and degrees, play a pivotal role. However, the unique challenges posed by DDoS attacks—and particularly those leveraging IoT devices—require specialized courses that are often best delivered through hands-on workshops and real-world simulations. These immersive experiences bridge the theoretical with the practical, equipping learners with the skills to anticipate and mitigate DDoS attacks.

Simulated cyber ranges represent the cutting edge of cybersecurity training. These virtual environments allow for the safe replication of DDoS scenarios, providing a sandbox in which strategies can be tested and refined without risking actual infrastructure. By incorporating IoT scenarios into these simulations, cybersecurity professionals can gain invaluable insights into the complex dynamics of modern DDoS attacks, including the identification of subtle signs of a looming attack and the deployment of countermeasures in real-time.

Beyond formal training, fostering a culture of security awareness within organizations is paramount. Regular security briefings, updates on the latest threats, and tips for maintaining personal cybersecurity hygiene can cultivate an environment where every employee acts as a custodian of digital security. This culture is particularly crucial in mitigating the risks associated with IoT devices, many of which may be introduced into networks by employees without an understanding of the potential vulnerabilities they carry.

The complexity and diversity of DDoS threats necessitate a collaborative approach to cybersecurity education. Platforms for knowledge sharing—ranging from online forums and webinars to international conferences—can facilitate a collective defense strategy. Through these collaborations, insights into emerging threats can be shared rapidly and best practices disseminated, strengthening the global response to DDoS attacks.

as the landscape of cyber warfare continues to evolve, the role of training and education in preparing for and responding to DDoS attacks cannot be overstated. From the intricacies of defending against IoT-driven attacks to the broader principles of cybersecurity, a well-informed and continuously educated workforce stands as the bulwark against the ever-present threat of digital assault. As we look to the future, investing in cybersecurity education is not just a strategy for defense but an imperative for ensuring the resilience and integrity of our digital world.

The Importance of Cybersecurity Education and Training

Cybersecurity education and training are instrumental in shifting the paradigm from a reactive to a proactive stance on cyber threats. Traditional approaches often focus on responding to breaches after they occur. In contrast, a comprehensive educational framework empowers individuals and organizations to anticipate, identify, and neutralize threats before they manifest into full-blown attacks. This proactive posture is particularly crucial in countering DDoS attacks, where the speed and scale of the response can significantly mitigate the impact.

At the heart of effective cybersecurity education lies the dual focus on technical competency and critical thinking. While technical skills provide the tools necessary to implement security measures, critical thinking enables individuals to analyze and adapt to the ever-changing tactics of cyber adversaries. Training programs designed with this dual focus prepare cybersecurity professionals to tackle DDoS attacks not just with technical solutions but with strategic foresight, analyzing patterns and predicting potential vulnerabilities.

The global landscape of cybersecurity is marked by a profound skills gap, with a significant shortage of qualified professionals to counter the rising tide of cyber threats. By prioritizing cybersecurity education and training, we can bridge this gap, creating a robust pipeline of skilled individuals ready to take on the challenges posed by DDoS attacks and other cyber threats. This effort extends beyond formal education institutions and into the realms of professional development and continuous learning, ensuring that the current workforce remains adept and agile in the face of new challenges.

Cybersecurity is not a solitary endeavor but a collective one, where shared knowledge and collaborative defense strategies play a pivotal role. Cybersecurity education and training programs that emphasize collaboration—through team-based projects, shared cyber ranges, and inter-organizational exercises —cultivate a sense of shared responsibility. This collaborative ethos is particularly effective against DDoS attacks, which often target wide networks and require coordinated responses from multiple stakeholders.

Beyond the organizational level, cybersecurity education and training play a crucial role in empowering individuals with the knowledge and practices of cyber hygiene. From recognizing phishing attempts to securing personal devices, these practices are the foundational blocks of a secure digital space. As DDoS attacks increasingly leverage compromised personal devices to amplify their impact, educating the wider public on cyber hygiene becomes an indispensable strategy in the broader fight against cyber threats.

The importance of cybersecurity education and training cannot be overstated. It is the keystone of cyber resilience, underpinning every effort to safeguard digital assets against the onslaught of DDoS attacks and other cyber threats. As we navigate the complexities of the digital age, our commitment to cybersecurity education and training will determine not just our ability to respond to threats, but our capacity to envision a secure digital future. Through dedication to continuous learning and adaptation, we arm ourselves with the most potent weapon against cyber threats: knowledge.

Resources for Continuous Learning and Professional Development

Online learning platforms have emerged as a cornerstone for cybersecurity education, offering a wealth of courses that span from introductory levels to advanced specializations. Platforms such as Coursera, edX, and Udemy provide access to courses created by leading universities and cybersecurity organizations. These courses often cover a range of topics crucial for understanding and combating DDoS attacks, including network security, encryption methodologies, and cyber defense strategies. The flexibility of online learning allows professionals to advance at their own pace, accommodating the relentless demands of cybersecurity roles.

Certifications play a pivotal role in the professional development of cybersecurity experts. Renowned certifications such as Certified Information Systems Security Professional (CISSP),

Certified Ethical Hacker (CEH), and Cisco's CCNA Cyber Ops not only validate an individual's expertise but also provide a structured learning path through the vast cybersecurity domain. These certifications often require participants to engage with materials and scenarios that mirror real-world challenges, including the mitigation and prevention of DDoS attacks.

Cyber ranges are virtual environments that simulate real-world IT infrastructure, allowing cybersecurity professionals to practice responding to various cyber threats, including DDoS attacks, in a controlled setting. Platforms like Cyberbit and the National Cyber Range Complex offer scenarios that range from basic threat identification to complex, multi-layered cyber-attack simulations. These environments are invaluable for honing the practical skills needed to effectively counteract and mitigate cyber threats.

Attending industry conferences, seminars, and webinars is another crucial avenue for continuous learning. Events such as DEF CON, Black Hat, and the RSA Conference provide unique opportunities for cybersecurity professionals to learn from peers, industry leaders, and innovators. These events often feature sessions and workshops specifically focusing on DDoS attack trends, mitigation strategies, and the latest in cyber defense technologies, enabling attendees to expand their knowledge and network with fellow professionals.

Communities and forums offer an interactive platform for cybersecurity professionals to exchange knowledge, share experiences, and seek advice on specific challenges. Platforms like Stack Exchange's Information Security, Reddit's r/cybersecurity, and InfoSec Forums are rich with discussions on the latest threats, including DDoS attacks, and the most effective defense strategies. Participation in these communities can provide valuable insights, foster professional relationships, and keep professionals abreast of emerging trends and solutions.

For those inclined towards in-depth research and academic rigor, journals and publications serve as an excellent resource. Publications like the Journal of Cybersecurity and Privacy, Computers & Security, and the International Journal of Information Security offer peer-reviewed articles on cutting-edge research, case studies on DDoS attacks, and analyses of new defense mechanisms. Engaging with these publications can deepen understanding and inspire innovative approaches to cybersecurity challenges.

The path to excellence in the cybersecurity field is paved with a commitment to continuous learning and professional development. By leveraging the vast array of resources available —from online courses and certifications to cyber ranges and industry events—cybersecurity professionals can stay ahead in the perpetual race against cyber threats like DDoS attacks. This ongoing journey of education and skill refinement is not just a professional obligation; it is the essence of resilience and effectiveness in the cybersecurity domain.

Building a Community of Cybersecurity Professionals for Knowledge Exchange

The foundation of a vibrant cybersecurity community lies in the creation of both virtual and physical spaces that facilitate interaction, dialogue, and collaboration. Online platforms, including LinkedIn groups, specialized forums, and dedicated Slack channels, offer accessible venues for continuous engagement. Meanwhile, local meetups, hackathons, and workshops provide invaluable opportunities for face-to-face interaction, fostering a sense of camaraderie and mutual support that strengthens the community's fabric.

The power of a community is magnified when its members actively contribute to and benefit from a shared repository of knowledge. Platforms such as GitHub and GitLab have become pivotal in this regard, hosting open-source projects and collaborative endeavors that address cybersecurity challenges. By contributing to these projects, professionals not only enhance their skills but also contribute to the development of robust, community-vetted solutions to complex problems such as DDoS mitigation techniques.

Mentorship is a cornerstone of professional development within the cybersecurity community. Experienced practitioners mentoring newcomers help in transferring tacit knowledge that is often not captured in textbooks or courses. Such relationships can be facilitated through formal mentorship programs organized by professional associations or informally within organizations and online communities. Peer support groups also play a crucial role, offering a platform for sharing experiences, challenges, and successes, thus accelerating collective learning and resilience.

Capture-The-Flag (CTF) competitions epitomize the gamification of cybersecurity learning and skill enhancement. These contests challenge participants to solve security-related puzzles and perform tasks ranging from penetration testing to cryptanalysis and code exploitation. By organizing or participating in CTF events, professionals not only sharpen their skills but also foster a spirit of competition and collaboration that is central to the ethos of the cybersecurity community.

The cybersecurity field is rapidly evolving, with new threats and technologies emerging at an unprecedented pace.

Community-driven research and development projects offer a pathway for professionals to engage in cutting-edge innovation. Collaborations across academia, industry, and government can lead to breakthroughs in DDoS defense strategies, encryption methods, and cyber threat detection algorithms. These projects not only advance the state of cybersecurity but also provide participants with exposure to diverse perspectives and challenges.

The endeavor to build a community of cybersecurity professionals is akin to erecting a fortress with knowledge as its foundation and collaboration as its walls. Within this fortress, the exchange of wisdom, the nurturing of talents, and the forging of alliances converge to create a formidable defense against the multifaceted threats of the digital age, including the ever-present menace of DDoS attacks. By investing in the growth and cohesion of this community, we not only enhance individual capabilities but also elevate the collective capacity to safeguard our interconnected world.

Building Resilient Systems and Networks

In the digital amphitheater of modern civilization, where the specters of cyber threats loom large and unyielding, the construction of resilient systems and networks represents a bulwark of paramount importance. This segment delves into the principles and practices instrumental in forging infrastructures capable of withstanding the onslaught of Distributed Denial of Service (DDoS) attacks, thereby ensuring continuity, integrity, and availability of services in the face of adversities.

The blueprint for resilience in cybersecurity is predicated on the philosophy of designing systems and networks that are not only robust but also adaptable to the ever-evolving landscape

TAKEHIRO KANEGI

of threats. This involves embracing a multi-layered approach to security, incorporating redundant systems, and deploying failover mechanisms that guarantee service continuity even when parts of the network are compromised or under attack.

At the heart of a resilient architecture lies the concept of redundancy—having multiple, interchangeable components that can take over functions in case of failure. This is complemented by failover strategies, which ensure seamless transition between primary and backup systems with minimal disruption. Implementing such mechanisms requires meticulous planning and testing to cover various failure scenarios, from hardware malfunctions to sophisticated DDoS attacks.

Diversification is another cornerstone of resilience, serving as a countermeasure against attacks targeting specific network paths or providers. By routing traffic through multiple paths and employing services from different Internet Service Providers (ISPs), organizations can mitigate the risk of a single point of failure. This strategy not only enhances the robustness of the network but also provides flexibility in response to attacks, allowing for dynamic rerouting of traffic to minimize impact.

In the arms race against cyber adversaries, static defenses are invariably outmaneuvered. Adaptive security measures, which evolve in real-time based on threat intelligence and ongoing risk assessments, form the vanguard of a resilient defense. This adaptive approach encompasses automated responses to attacks, machine learning algorithms for anomaly detection, and continuous updates to security policies and configurations.

Artificial intelligence (AI) and machine learning (ML) technologies have emerged as potent allies in the quest for resilience. By analyzing patterns and predicting potential threats, these technologies can preemptively identify and mitigate DDoS attacks before they escalate. Furthermore, AI and ML can optimize the allocation of resources during an attack, ensuring that critical services remain unaffected.

Proactive threat hunting involves actively searching for signs of compromise or vulnerabilities within systems and networks before they can be exploited by attackers. This proactive stance not only aids in early detection of threats but also contributes to a deeper understanding of the attack landscape, informing the development of more effective defense measures.

Building resilient systems and networks is not a solitary endeavor but a collective pursuit. Collaboration among organizations, sharing of threat intelligence, and participation in cybersecurity alliances enhance the collective resilience against DDoS attacks. By pooling resources and knowledge, the cybersecurity community can craft more robust defenses, benefiting all members through shared insights and coordinated response strategies.

The edifice of resilience is perpetually under construction, demanding ongoing vigilance, innovation, and commitment. In the shadow of the DDoS threat, building resilient systems and networks is both a shield and a testament to the indomitable spirit of those who safeguard the digital domain. Through the concerted efforts of designing with redundancy, adapting to new threats, and fostering collaboration, the cybersecurity community fortifies its defenses, ensuring that the vital functions of our interconnected society endure.

Long-term Strategies for Building Resilient Infrastructures

In the evolving tableau of cyber warfare, the imperative to construct resilient infrastructures cannot be overstated. This discourse elucidates on the long-term strategies essential for crafting infrastructures that not only resist the immediate threats of Distributed Denial of Service (DDoS) attacks but also adapt to the shifting paradigms of cyber threats over time. These strategies are the bedrock upon which the future security posture of organizations will rest, ensuring that their digital assets and services remain unassailable amidst the tumult of the cyber realm.

The foundation of resilient infrastructures is predicated on a culture of security that permeates every level of an organization. This culture is characterized by the recognition of cybersecurity as a critical business function, and not merely a technical concern. It advocates for the inclusion of security considerations in the earliest stages of infrastructure design and throughout the lifecycle of systems and networks. Such a culture fosters proactive security practices, continuous learning, and adaptation to new threats.

Risk assessment and management form the continuous backbone of resilient infrastructures. By regularly evaluating the threat landscape and the organization's exposure to these threats, security teams can prioritize resources and efforts to address the most critical vulnerabilities. This dynamic approach to risk management entails not only the identification and mitigation of risks but also the preparation for and recovery from potential breaches, ensuring a swift return to normal operations.

The architectural design of resilient infrastructures relies on principles that enhance their ability to withstand and recover from attacks. These principles include:

- Segmentation: Dividing the network into smaller, manageable segments that can isolate incidents and contain breaches.

- Least Privilege: Ensuring that entities (users, services, devices) have only the access necessary to perform their functions, reducing the potential impact of compromised credentials or systems.

- Zero Trust: Operating under the assumption that threats can originate from both outside and within the network, thereby enforcing strict access controls and verification at every step.

The rapid advancement of technology offers a plethora of tools and solutions for enhancing resilience. Investment in these technologies should be strategic, with a focus on solutions that offer long-term value. These include:

- Sophisticated Monitoring and Analytics: Tools that provide real-time visibility into network traffic and behavior, enabling the early detection of anomalies that could indicate a DDoS attack.

- Automation and Orchestration: Solutions that automate the response to detected threats, reducing the time to mitigation and freeing human resources for more complex analysis and decision-making.

- Cloud-based and Hybrid Solutions: Leveraging the scalability and flexibility of cloud services to distribute and absorb attack traffic, while hybrid models ensure redundancy and continuity.

The complexity and sophistication of DDoS attacks necessitate a collaborative approach to resilience. Organizations should engage in information-sharing initiatives, both within their industry and across sectors. Participating in forums, working groups, and alliances allows for the exchange of threat intelligence, best practices, and coordinated responses to emerging threats. This collective wisdom enriches an organization's security posture and contributes to the larger goal of cyber resilience.

CHAPTER 9:
PREPARING FOR
THE FUTURE

Anticipating future challenges is essential for maintaining resilient infrastructures. This involves staying abreast of emerging technologies, understanding their potential security implications, and adapting strategies accordingly. It also means preparing for the increasing interconnectedness of systems and the proliferation of Internet of Things (IoT) devices, which will introduce new vulnerabilities and attack vectors.

Building resilient infrastructures is a journey that demands foresight, adaptability, and a steadfast commitment to security as a core organizational value. By cultivating a security-conscious culture, implementing continuous risk management, adhering to architectural principles, investing in advanced technologies, and fostering collaboration, organizations can fortify their defenses against the DDoS threats of today and tomorrow. The path to resilience is paved with challenges, but through concerted effort and strategic planning, the integrity and availability of critical digital services can be preserved.

Incorporating Resiliency Planning into Business and Development Processes

In the modern business landscape, where digital infrastructure forms the backbone of operations, the integration of resiliency planning into business and development processes emerges as a non-negotiable imperative. This narrative delves into the methodologies and frameworks that fortify an organization's capability to endure and swiftly recover from Distributed Denial of Service (DDoS) attacks, thereby safeguarding continuity and service integrity.

The first stride towards embedding resiliency into the organizational fabric requires a harmonization of business objectives with resiliency goals. This alignment ensures that the pursuit of robustness against cyber threats advances in tandem with business growth strategies. Leadership commitment is crucial, as it drives the prioritization of resources and fosters an environment where resilience is viewed as an indispensable element of business success.

The infusion of resiliency planning within the development life cycle is pivotal. Adopting a resilience-by-design approach, where security and continuity measures are not afterthoughts but are integral from the inception of a project, significantly reduces vulnerabilities and enhances the system's ability to withstand and recover from attacks. This approach encompasses:

- Threat Modeling: Early and ongoing analysis of potential threats to identify and address vulnerabilities within the development phase.

- Resilient Architectural Design: Implementation of design principles that promote redundancy, failover capabilities, and graceful degradation to ensure service continuity.

- Security and Resilience Testing: Rigorous testing regimes that simulate DDoS scenarios to evaluate the system's response and refine its resilience posture.

Operational procedures must evolve to incorporate resilience strategies effectively. This includes the establishment of incident response teams and protocols that are specifically tailored to manage and mitigate the impact of DDoS attacks. Training and drills play a critical role, ensuring that when an actual incident occurs, the response is swift, coordinated, and effective, minimizing downtime and operational disruption.

A resilient organization is one that learns and adapts. The implementation of feedback loops that capture learnings from incidents and testing exercises is vital. This mechanism enables the continual refinement of resilience strategies, ensuring they remain effective against the backdrop of an ever-evolving threat landscape. It also encourages a culture of openness and learning, where insights derived from near-misses and successful mitigations inform future planning.

The complexity of DDoS attacks and the sophistication required to defend against them necessitate the leverage of cutting-edge technologies and strategic partnerships. Collaboration with cloud service providers, cybersecurity firms, and industry consortiums can extend an organization's capability to detect, respond to, and recover from DDoS incidents. Technologies such as machine learning can provide predictive capabilities, identifying anomalous patterns that may signify an impending attack, enabling pre-emptive action.

Incorporating resiliency planning into business and development processes also means adhering to regulatory requirements and industry best practices. Compliance not only avoids legal repercussions but also serves as a guideline for establishing robust cybersecurity and resilience frameworks. The adherence to standards such as ISO/IEC 27001 and frameworks like NIST can provide a structured approach to managing cybersecurity risks and enhancing resilience.

The essence of incorporating resiliency planning into business and development processes transcends mere technical and procedural adjustments. It demands the cultivation of a resilience culture that permeates every layer of the organization. From the boardroom to the development teams, there must be a unified commitment to safeguarding the organization's digital estate against DDoS threats through strategic planning, continuous improvement, and collaboration. This holistic approach not only protects the organization but also affirms its reliability and commitment to its customers and stakeholders in an unpredictable digital age.

Importance of Collaboration Between Tech Companies, Governments, and NGOs to Combat DDoS Threats

Tech companies are at the forefront of innovation in cybersecurity, developing sophisticated solutions to detect, mitigate, and prevent DDoS attacks. Their expertise in cutting-edge technologies, including artificial intelligence (AI) and machine learning, offers valuable tools for identifying and neutralizing threats. Governments, on the other hand, possess authoritative capabilities and resources to enforce laws, regulate cyberspace, and facilitate international cooperation. NGOs contribute through advocacy, research, and education, raising awareness about cybersecurity threats and best practices. By pooling their unique strengths and resources, these entities can create a robust defense mechanism against DDoS attacks that neither could achieve independently.

One of the pillars of effective DDoS defense is the timely sharing of threat intelligence. Tech companies often detect emerging threats through their networks, while governments may have access to intelligence about cybercriminal activities. NGOs, with their broad outreach, can disseminate this information to raise awareness and preparedness among stakeholders. Establishing formal and informal channels for information exchange enables the rapid dissemination of threat indicators, enhancing the collective ability to preempt attacks or respond swiftly when they occur.

The complexity and scale of DDoS attacks often exceed the capacity of any single organization to respond effectively. A coordinated response strategy, involving tech companies, government agencies, and NGOs, ensures a comprehensive approach to mitigating the impact of attacks. This could include tech companies deploying countermeasures, government agencies managing crisis communication and legal actions against perpetrators, and NGOs supporting affected communities. Such collaboration facilitates a unified and effective response, minimizing the damage and restoring normal operations more rapidly.

Collaboration between tech companies, governments, and NGOs is pivotal in the development and implementation of cybersecurity policies and standards. Governments can enact policies that mandate security practices to protect against DDoS attacks, drawing on the technical insight of tech companies and the societal perspectives of NGOs. Together, they can advocate for the adoption of international standards and agreements that promote cybersecurity and deter cybercrime, creating a safer digital environment for all.

The perpetually evolving nature of DDoS threats necessitates ongoing research and development (R&D) to stay ahead of attackers. Joint R&D initiatives can leverage the technological prowess of the private sector, the policy-making capacity of governments, and the community outreach of NGOs. By working together, these sectors can accelerate the development of innovative DDoS defense mechanisms and strategies, ensuring they are effective against the latest threats and widely adopted across different segments of society.

The battle against DDoS threats cannot be won in isolation. It requires the concerted efforts of tech companies, governments, and NGOs, each bringing their unique capabilities to the table. Through collaboration, these entities can fortify the digital landscape against DDoS attacks, safeguarding the integrity of online services and the privacy of individuals. Standing united, the global community can build a resilient digital future, where cybersecurity is a shared responsibility and a common goal.

ADDITIONAL RESOURCES

Books

1. "Cybersecurity – Attack and Defense Strategies" by Yuri Diogenes and Erdal Ozkaya - This book offers a deep dive into cybersecurity strategies, including defending against DDoS attacks.

2. "Network Security Essentials: Applications and Standards" by William Stallings - Provides a solid foundation in network security, including techniques to combat DDoS attacks.

3. "Practical Packet Analysis: Using Wireshark to Solve Real-World Network Problems" by Chris Sanders - A hands-on guide to understanding network traffic and spotting anomalies that could indicate a DDoS attack.

Articles

1. "The Growing DDoS Threat: What You Need to Know" by CSO Online - An insightful article on the evolving landscape of DDoS attacks and trends.

2. "Understanding DDoS Attacks" by Cloudflare - Offers a comprehensive overview of how DDoS attacks work and ways to mitigate them.

3. "DDoS Attack Definitions, DDoS Mitigation, and DDoS Attack Prevention" by Imperva - A detailed article explaining DDoS attack strategies and prevention methods.

Websites

1. Cloudflare Learning Center (https://www.cloudflare.com/learning/) - A repository of articles covering DDoS attacks and cybersecurity practices.

2. Krebs on Security (https://krebsonsecurity.com/) - A leading resource on cybersecurity, including analysis of DDoS attacks and defenses.

3. DDoS Mitigation Guide (https://www.us-cert.gov/ncas/tips/ST04-015) - A guide from the United States Computer Emergency Readiness Team.

Organizations

1. The Center for Internet Security (CIS) (https://www.cisecurity.org/) - Offers resources and benchmarks to improve the security posture of organizations vulnerable to DDoS attacks.

2. Electronic Frontier Foundation (EFF) (https://www.eff.org/) - Provides insights into legal and technical aspects of defending against DDoS attacks.

3. Internet Society (https://www.internetsociety.org/) - Focuses on policies, technology, and development to ensure an open and secure internet, including defenses against DDoS attacks.

Tools

1. Wireshark (https://www.wireshark.org/) - A network protocol analyzer that can be used for real-time network analysis, including detecting DDoS attack patterns.

2. DDoS Detection & Mitigation Tools by Arbor Networks - Offers a range of products designed to detect and mitigate DDoS attacks in real-time.

3. Cloudflare (https://www.cloudflare.com/) - Provides a comprehensive DDoS protection service that can safeguard websites, applications, and entire networks.

4. Akamai Prolexic Solutions (https://www.akamai.com/) - Delivers scalable DDoS mitigation solutions for high-volume attacks.

www.ingramcontent.com/pod-product-compliance
Lightning Source LLC
Chambersburg PA
CBHW071110050326
40690CB00008B/1180